A Freelancer's Survival Guide to Reaching Your Goals

The Freelancer's Survival Guide

Getting Started, When to Quit Your Day Job and *Networking in Person and Online* are just a few chapters from *The Freelancer's Survival Guide*, a 612-page "bible for the self-employed." Don't miss a single tip. Available in ebook, trade paperback and audiobook from your favorite bookseller.

A Freelancer's Survival Guide to Reaching Your Goals

Kristine Kathryn Rusch

A Freelancer's Survival Guide to Reaching Your Goals
Copyright © 2020 by Kristine Kathryn Rusch
Published by WMG Publishing
Layout and design © copyright 2020 WMG Publishing
Cover design by Allyson Longueira/WMG Publishing
Cover art © copyright Olivier26/Depositphotos
ISBN-13: 978-1-56146-703-7
ISBN-10: 1-56146-703-0

Time Management
Copyright © 2018 by Kristine Kathryn Rusch
First published in 2009 and 2010 in slightly different versions on kristinekathrynrusch.com.
Published by WMG Publishing
Layout and design © copyright 2018 WMG Publishing
Cover design by Allyson Longueira/WMG Publishing
Cover art © copyright Siarhei Hashnikau/Dreamstime

Turning Setbacks Into Opportunities
Copyright © 2018 by Kristine Kathryn Rusch
First published in 2009 and 2010 in slightly different versions on kristinekathrynrusch.com
Published by WMG Publishing
Layout and design © copyright 2018 WMG Publishing
Cover design by Allyson Longueira/WMG Publishing
Cover art © copyright Iqoncept/Dreamstime

Goals & Dreams
Copyright © 2018 by Kristine Kathryn Rusch
Published by WMG Publishing
Layout and design © copyright 2018 WMG Publishing
Cover design by Allyson Longueira/WMG Publishing
Cover art © copyright Leo Blanchette/Dreamstime

All rights reserved.
No part of this book may be reproduced in any form or by any electronic or mechanical means, including information storage and retrieval systems, without written permission from the author, except for the use of brief quotations in a book review.

Contents

Time Management

Introduction	5
Time	7
Schedules and How to Keep Them	17
Deadlines	29
Discipline	37
Illness	51
Vacations	57

Turning Setbacks Into Opportunity

Introduction	73
Setbacks	75
Failure	99
The Benefits of Hindsight	107

Goals & Dreams

Introduction	123
The Difference Between Goals And Dreams	125
Patience	133
Expectations	141
Giving Up On Yourself	153
Staying Positive	169
Reaching For Your Dreams	181
About the Author	193

TIME MANAGEMENT

A FREELANCER'S SURVIVAL GUIDE
SHORT BOOK

The key to a successful freelance career lies in time management. This short book examines all the important elements of time management, including scheduling your day, meeting your deadlines, and knowing when to take a vacation.

Introduction

The hardest thing for first-time freelancers to do is manage their time. It sounds easy, right? You figure out what you need to get done, and then you do it. You have all day. After all, you don't have to drive to a day job.

But it's not easy. The first six months of freelancing are often the least productive of your entire career. In those six months, you reinvent the wheel when it comes to time management. You figure out what gets in the way of your work (and it's usually you), then you solve that problem, and then you move on to the next.

There are other issues, as well. When are you too sick to work? When do you take a vacation? *Should* you take a vacation? Isn't your work a vacation...from a day job?

Then there are deadlines, schedules, and family members to organize yourself around. If you're not good at saying no, you'll have trouble with time management.

This short book has a lot of tips to help you schedule your time and yourself. It covers everything from discipline to deadlines, vacations to scheduling each moment of your day.

Time Management is part of a series of short books excerpted from my longer work, *The Freelancer's Survival Guide*. I wrote the *Guide* on my blog, kristinekathrynrusch.com. Each segment of this

INTRODUCTION

book came from a blog post, some of which I've altered and some I've left as is. If you want to see what else is in the *Guide*, or look at the original versions of the posts (along with the comments), go to my website and click on the *Freelancer's Survival Guide* tab. There you will find the table of contents.

Or you can buy the entire *Guide* in paper or electronic form. But I know that some of you need help in only a few areas, so the entire *Guide* might be full of too much information. That's why I've broken certain sections, like this one, into a short book. There are several other short books, including books on *How To Make Money* and *When To Quit Your Day Job*. You'll find a complete list at the beginning and end of this book or on my website under the electronic books/nonfiction tab.

The time you spend reading this short book should help you save time in the future. Thanks for buying the book—and good luck with your freelance career.

—Kristine Kathryn Rusch
Lincoln City, Oregon
August 27, 2010

TIME

Time. That's what any business boils down to. Time. I learned this quite young. I got paid by the hour (by the minute, really) at my very first long-term job as a waitress. That time clock, with its time stamp, tracked every single moment I was on the job. If I clocked in at 6:05 a.m. and clocked out at 1:55 p.m., I did not work eight hours. I worked seven hours and fifty minutes, and that's what I got paid for.

I really learned the meaning of time when I worked in radio. Everything in broadcast news is measured in seconds. Years later, after I became a science fiction writer, a television interviewer pulled me aside and said in surprise, "You're the first writer I've met who speaks in thirty-second sound bites."

Gosh, guess where I learned that.

I also learned to watch the clock. If the news had to be on at seven, you couldn't be five minutes late. It was seven or there would be the catastrophe of catastrophes—dead air.

Time isn't just about deadlines. Time is about efficiency. You see, we're only allowed so many hours on this Earth. In fact, Clint Black has a great song about this phenomenon called "No Time To Kill," which I'd quote to you if there weren't copyright issues preventing it. No matter what we do, we don't get additional hours. Our days are 24 hours long, no matter what. The week lasts for seven days, no matter how hard we try to change that.

We can shortchange other parts of our lives to get more time. We can sleep less, spend less time with friends, or give up things we love, but those are only short-term solutions. If you do that for too long, you'll blow. You'll either get sick or have some kind of breakdown or (my explosion of choice) quit whatever it is that has taken all your time in a loud and dramatic fashion.

The best way to "gain" more time is to use what time you have more efficiently. There are a wide variety of ways to do that.

Here are some of the most common:

1. Work harder.

Years ago, a friend of mine who manages an entire division in a corporation told me that corporations factor in worker downtime. In other words (and I'm making up the statistics here, being too lazy to look them up), corporations figure that for every hour an employee is at the job, he works only forty minutes. The rest of the time is spent on the phone or in the bathroom or gossiping with coworkers. So in an eight-hour day, a corporate employee probably only works 5.3 hours.

When you work for yourself, there's no one to track your productivity. You can goof off until bedtime if you want—and newer at-home professionals often do. You think you have an entire day, and suddenly that entire day has gone by.

It's especially easy these days to waste time and feel productive while doing so. Twitter, Facebook, e-mail, and surfing the web feel like writing work to me, but if I spend all day typing Tweets and long letters to friends, I'm not getting any paying work done. Yet I've been writing all day long.

This is why I have no Internet access whatsoever in my office. I won't even allow myself to bring my nifty new iPhone in here because that way lies inefficiency and financial death.

I have a separate office for everything that is not writing, from my phone to my laptop with its wireless Internet connection to my television with its online capability.

In fact, over the years, I've weeded all distractions out of my office, like games on my computer and other people's fiction. Now if I want to waste time, I have to leave my office—a real clear sign that I'm not doing my job.

2. Work smarter.

This was the category that initially worried me as I wrote *The Freelancer's Survival Guide* on my blog. I couldn't write it any faster than any of my other projects. So I hoped that in the future all of the time I spent on the *Guide* would pay off.

As the *Guide* progressed, I had some intangible results, ones that matter. More people than ever now come to my website, and many are unfamiliar with my fiction. I get several letters per week from folks who've read the *Guide* who are now going to pick up a novel that I've written. So I'm gaining an added benefit here, one I didn't expect. I'm writing something that's turning into a loss leader.

A loss leader, for those of you unfamiliar with the term, refers to something a business gives away or sells at a discount that will bring customers to the business. I did not expect the *Guide* to be a loss leader.

Nor, honestly, did I expect it to generate much money in the website form. I initially wrote the *Guide* for people to read immediately because the recession was forcing a lot of people to go to work for themselves before they're ready. I'm trying to help with that.

So when I started the *Guide*, I fully expected it to be a complete waste of time and money (for me). I looked at it the way I look at the volunteer work I've done: as something I'm giving back to the community, not as something that will bring me any benefits.

The fact that there are benefits surprises me immensely.

And there have been a lot of benefits besides the ones

mentioned above. I've learned about web publishing. WMG Publishing picked up the *Guide* and the short books excerpted from the larger volume. I made my advance off the website alone, and I have a new column, one that also talks about business and is called, appropriately, Business Rusch, which keeps the *Guide* going. The time wasn't wasted after all.

Let's assume, however, that the *Guide* wasn't an experiment for me. Let's assume that it was something I had done before, like most of my fiction is. I would have done what most businesses call a cost-benefit analysis.

If I spend x time on this project, I should get y benefit from the project. Together x and y should equal or exceed z. If x and y together are less than z, then the project is not worth doing.

Let's put this in more concrete terms. If I spend a week writing a short story, and receive $100 plus publication in a reputable magazine, is that worth my time? Not usually. Because if I spent one week writing and only get $100 for my work, then I'm earning $2.50 per hour, which is well under minimum wage. The less tangible benefits would have to be off the chart for me to work for that amount of money. Honestly, I can't even think of what those off-the-chart benefits could possibly be for me to work so long for so little money.

One writer friend of mine, a long-time professional, told me that if he wasn't earning a minimum of $500 per day on his writing, he had a bad day. Imagine what his response would be if someone asked him to spend a week writing a $100 short story.

I have my own hourly number, under which I generally do not take a project. That hourly number often includes a pain-in-the-ass tax. In other words, I'll work for some difficult clients but my fee is double or triple what it would be for other more easygoing folks.

I also factor in time. I'll take a lower-paying job than some writers because I'm a fast writer. I'll finish a project four times faster than most writers because of my broadcast training. I get things done. What this means is—to keep with our example—if someone asks me for a short story and can only pay me $100, I'll do a gut check. Does the story interest me? Yes. Do I want to be in that market? Yes. Can I write the story in an hour or two? If the answer to that final question is yes, then I'll take the project.

Often, however, the lowest paying clients are the ones who demand the most work.

So you, the professional, must work smarter. You must factor in *all* of the benefits for each job and then give a realistic estimate of your time. If the tangibles and the intangibles add up to something greater than it would appear at first glance, then take the project. But if they mean that you'd be short-changing yourself either in money or in time or in reputation, then turn the project down.

Here's the flipside. I've turned down projects that seem—on the surface—to be high-paying, surefire winners. I've watched the writers who've taken those projects suffer and lose money.

What happened?

Usually the pain-in-the-ass factor. The project, which should have taken three months, took three years. Three awful years of full manuscript revisions, four-hour conference calls that accomplished nothing, and a lot of wasted work. (Not to mention the hair-pulling agony of redoing a task over and over again for an unappreciative client.)

Nowadays, I can see these projects coming. I know which one will be a headache and which one won't. I've been doing this, as I said, for more than twenty years.

But I learned how to see these projects clearly because I made the mistake of taking some of them. I've suffered through them, and learned my lesson. I've learned that it's better to take the $5,000 project that requires two weeks of work than it is to take the $50,000 project that will suck two years from my life. You do the math. It's really not that hard, when you think about it.

In order to work smarter, you need to know what you want from your business and/or from each project that you do. For example, I want several things from my business. I want to continue my writing career. But I want to do it on my terms. I don't want to be a writer-for-hire, someone who writes what other people want.

Nor do I want to be constrained by expectations (I don't want to be pigeon-holed).

I want to continue funding my business. It must pay for itself and pay for my own living expenses.

I want to continue living in this little resort town by the sea, in my lovely home, with my wonderful husband. This life here in this little town costs me a certain amount of money every month—just like your life in your hometown costs you a certain amount of money every month.

So I have a monthly nut—the amount it takes me to live every single month. Multiply by twelve months in the year, then divide by 52. I now know what I must earn each week. (That's easier than trying to figure out if there are 4.5 weeks in a month or 4.3 or 4...) If I divide that weekly number by 40, then I know how much I must earn per hour, if I work a 40-hour week.

I now know what my hourly wage is. Then I must accurately figure out how much time each project will take. Take the amount that the project pays, and divide it by the number of hours it'll take you to finish that project. If you will earn your hourly wage plus some, take the project. If you will earn less than your hourly wage, turn the project down.

That's a simple formula, which you can adjust for intangibles such as bringing more people to your website. But if all of your projects pay mostly in intangibles, you won't earn enough to pay your bills.

Let's go back to the 5K/50K example.

Let's say you need $10 per hour to make your nut. (I know, most of you need a lot more, but $10 makes the math easy.) You figure the 5K project will take three weeks.

You need to earn $1200 to make your nut in three weeks. But for this three-week period of time, you'll earn $5000. Or to put it in hourly terms, you'll be earning $41 per hour when all you need is $10. That's $31 per hour *profit*.

But that 50K project: You thought it would only take one year, which means it'll pay off. You need to earn $20,800 in that year (52 weeks times 40 hours per week times $10 per hour). You'll make $50,000, more than double what you need. You'll earn $24 per hour—less than you'd earn on the short 5K project, but still good wages considering what you need to earn.

But if this 50K project extends over three years, then you will have lost $12,400 on this deal. (Your three-year nut is $62,400. You've earned only $50,000.) And we're talking if they paid up front. If the client pays the balance on completion, you might earn even less. Delayed payments cost you money in time and interest. Sometimes you don't even get the delayed payment, decreasing your pay rate even more.

Even if you got a lot of intangibles, such as good promotion and new clients coming to your business, they wouldn't make up for that devastating loss, which is more than a half a year's income.

Work smarter. Understand what each project will cost you in time, energy, and money.

3. Hire help.

I know, I know. In the *Freelancer's Survival Guide* online, I tell you not to hire an employee unless you need one.

But you might need one to help you become more efficient. Let's look at the 5K example. Let's assume you have one other project that also needs completion in that period of time. It pays $20 per hour and will take 60 hours total. That's an extra twenty hours during the week—so you'll have to work a 60-hour week for three weeks. Tough life.

Now let's assume that you must keep up this pace for the next six months. You can't afford a new employee at that rate, but you can afford someone to baby-sit the kids for a few hours during the week or someone to clean your house or cook your meals so that you're not constantly eating take-out.

Or maybe, like me, a 60-hour week doesn't scare you. But imagine if that stretches to an 80- or 100-hour week. At some point, you'll burn out. So you need to figure out how to cut your hours without losing income or clients.

Sometimes that means hiring a secretary or an assistant who comes in a few times per week. When the new owner of the collectibles store that my husband Dean Wesley Smith started realized that she needed to be onsite seven days per week, eight hours per day in this resort town's busy season plus put items on eBay in her off hours, she realized she couldn't handle all of that for the required five months. She brings in another employee one day per week, and has added a computer in the store, so that she can do eBay in her downtime.

She added a short-term employee for the season *and* decided to work smarter by adding eBay time into her store hours.

And that's what you have to do.

You need to figure out what your time is worth. You need to factor in the intangibles as well as the tangibles. (I don't take a lot of pain-in-the-ass projects; nor do I take projects that'll require me to leave home for months at a time.) You'll need to make sure you make your monthly nut plus some profit. And you'll need to factor in how much work you can actually do versus how much you think you can do.

(Usually self-employed people *overestimate* how much work they think they can do. They also overestimate how much work they think their employees can do, which leads to problems down the road.)

Here's the key to time: Make sure you get paid your hourly minimum on every single job. No exceptions. That way, you'll always pay your bills.

Defend your time. Make sure those around you understand that you're doing paying work in those hours.

And finally, if you work harder and smarter and still aren't making your monthly nut, then you need to reassess your business. Because something isn't working. Either you're taking the wrong projects for the wrong reasons or you're not getting enough good paying work.

Time Management

If you're doing this right, though, you should make a profit on most of your projects. People who know what their time is worth tend to do well in business.

Value your time. Charge for it.

You'll be glad you did.

Schedules and How to Keep Them

I often work with start-up publishers. I like their enthusiasm and their vision. After all, I once co-owned a start-up publishing company, as well.

However, because I co-owned such a company, I keep a careful eye on the start-ups. I make sure that I can get out of my contracts easily if need be.

When I see potential trouble in a start-up, I let the owner know. If the trouble doesn't get fixed, I do an assessment: can I live with that trouble? Will that trouble affect my work? If the answer to both of those questions is no, then I stay. If it's yes, I try once more to solve the problems, and if that fails, I leave.

Over the years, I have left primarily due to lack of payment. Start-ups run through their money quicker than anyone else. Several years ago, one start-up didn't have enough cash to publish an anthology I had contributed to. The owner sent a letter, saying payment would come six months after publication, which I found unacceptable. The owner, in other words, got all the benefit, and if that owner failed to pay, I would lose first publication rights to my story and never get compensated for them.

Besides, the owner violated the contract. I informed the owner of this, asked for my payment (which, supposedly on acceptance, was now overdue), and when the owner reiterated that no payment would come until six months after publication, I pulled the story. The book was already in production. That decision cost the publisher five times more than it would have if the publisher had simply honored our contract.

Such problems are common with start-ups. I've had to deal with at least one of these issues per year. The handwriting is always on the wall at that point. If the start-up delays payment, the start-up has money troubles. If a start-up has money troubles, *and continues to deny them*, the start-up will—and I mean *will*—go out of business.

In this particular case, the start-up I referred to was gone one year later. Half the authors in that anthology got their post-publication payment. The other half did not. The authors in the next anthology never did get paid.

Money issues are a place where problems become visible. Anyone who pays attention can see that handwriting on the wall.

But some time back, I had a different issue with a start-up. It had to do with scheduling.

This start-up—a small press—contracted to reissue several of my books. The editor who contacted me was one of the most reputable in the business. The press's owner had had a few business failures in the past, but I see that as a plus. The owner had managed to get start-up capital despite those failures. The owner also was a bright person who learned from mistakes. I think failure is a good thing, if a person can learn from it, so I did not hold the failures against the owner, but I made a wary note of them, just like I would have if there were hints of money troubles.

This company had no money troubles. It was drowning in capital and had great plans for various projects. But I had a lot of trouble finding out when my books would be published. My editor couldn't get answers on that issue either. And no one provided deadlines. I thought that strange.

Then came some personnel changes. My editor left. The new editor never answered e-mail. Neither did the owner. And I had some pretty serious questions that needed answering. Most importantly, I needed to know the publishing schedule because some of the books being reissued had co-publishing arrangements.

After months of no response from the publisher, I finally sent a registered letter canceling the contracts. I took longer than usual in doing so, simply because the problems seemed so unusual. But I was complaining to Dean one afternoon and I heard myself say this, "If I'm having trouble getting responses now before publication, when a publisher is *excited* about a project, imagine how hard it'll be to get a response if there's an actual problem, like a delayed payment or a botched cover."

That sentence decided me. I couldn't continue to do business with this publisher.

Eventually, the owner responded to my registered letter. The owner demanded to know why I hadn't e-mailed. I sent copies of all my correspondence. We had several backs and forths, and things seemed to be getting resolved. Then I reiterated that I needed the publishing schedule.

The owner asked me why I needed a schedule. I mentioned the co-publishing agreements, and then I stated what seemed obvious to me: All publishers had a schedule. This publisher just needed to share theirs with their authors.

"But," the publisher wrote back, "none of my companies have ever had any schedule, and we've done fine."

Suddenly, all became clear. The previous businesses hadn't failed from undercapitalization or from overextending. They had all failed because the owner had never *ever* had a schedule, and was now repeating the same mistake.

Needless to say, I stood by my cancellation, which turned out to be a good decision.

The poor business owner never did understand what had gone wrong, with me and with others. The company, while initially on solid financial footing, started having trouble. The troubles had nothing to do with the finances and everything to do with the lack of a schedule.

You see, without a schedule, other businesses can't work with yours. If you're a publisher, bookstores won't know when to order your books – and won't be able to depend on them to arrive on time. If you're a reader, you won't know when a book becomes available. Five novels arrived in the mail this week, all of which I had pre-ordered, all of them I have been looking forward to for *months* and in one case, *years*. The books arrived on time, and I'm a happy, if overwhelmed, fan.

If you're a busy author, like me, you need the schedule so that you can meet your deadlines. If you're familiar with publishing, you can also see when things start going awry. Many years ago, an inexperienced editor at a major U.S. publishing house forgot to put my book into production. I noticed when the copy edit was late, then when the proof didn't show. I—and several other authors—had our agents find out what was going on. What was going on was that this editor was very incompetent, and once writers and their representatives started complaining, this editor got fired. My book was delayed for a year because someone hadn't met the schedule.

This book, called *Hitler's Angel,* ended up with a 500-copy print run in the United States because bookstores got confused. Most bookstores rely on their computers to track orders. The computers told the stores that the stores had ordered the book a year before and sold no copies. (Apparently the computers don't mention whether or not the book actually arrives.) So no major bookstore ordered the book.

The editor's mistake cost me thousands and thousands of dollars and doomed a good book for thirteen years. In 2010, John Blake in England published *Hitler's Angel* properly, with a good print run, reviews, and oh yeah, an actual schedule. (The book also arrived in the U.S. via John Blake in 2011—according to the schedule.)

A solid publishing schedule gives the author all kinds of flexibility, and when an author is multipublished, keeps books spaced a proper length apart (or not, if we're jamming something for attention).

Time Management

Every publisher I've ever worked with, until this start-up, knew that a schedule was important. Not all publishers—particularly the new ones—could keep to the schedule, but they at least tried.

Recently, I had the happy surprise of encountering an extremely organized and scheduled publisher. I turned in a novel and got an e-mail from the managing editor, with all the important dates—when the revision (if there were any) was due, when the copy edits needed to be finished, when the proofs needed to be done, and when the book would be available for pre-order. I about fell off my chair with delight and surprise.

Then I picked myself up, compared this publication schedule to my personal schedule, and informed the company of a possible problem—I would be traveling for weeks when one of the due dates hit. We adjusted everything within the hour, and the managing editor told me this was why the company sent out the in-house schedule, so they could adjust it to accommodate everyone concerned.

Wow! Such professionalism. In twenty-plus years of publishing and being published, I had never encountered such specificity before. I loved it, and I confess, I feel spoiled now.

Now you know why schedules are so important to publishing. But what about other businesses? Do they need schedules?

Of course they do. Everyone needs a schedule. If you don't have a schedule, you end up like that poor start-up above. After I left that start-up, I continued to pay attention, and I watched that poor business owner run from one fire to another, always trying to put them out. Detail after detail got lost as problems blew up in the owner's face.

Schedules provide structure. Sometimes that structure is as simple as business hours posted on the door of a retail store. Customers know when the store is open, and the owner knows when she needs to be there. But the store needs to keep to the posted hours. After a few tries, customers won't return to a store that's closed during its posted hours.

Dean just encountered this. He needed a new computer and

since there's a recession going on, he wanted to give his money to a local store, even though it would have been easier to order the computer via the Internet. Dean told the owner he would show up on a particular Monday afternoon with a check. When Dean arrived, the store was closed. (A "Be Back Soon" sign was on the door.) Dean waited for twenty minutes, called the owner, got the store's answering machine, and gave up.

He left a message, informing the owner he had just lost a $2,000 sale, then came home and ordered the computer off the Internet. Weeks later, when Dean needed a cable for the computer, he tried the store again and found a different "Be Back Soon" sign. This time, he didn't wait. He went to another store ASAP, and will no longer return to this computer store.

The structure provides a framework for the entire business. It's up to the owner of the business to enforce that structure. For example, I recently heard of two different firings that occurred in our small town.

In the first, the employee showed up hours late for work, without calling. The employee did this repeatedly. After a year of this (!), the employee got fired. Was this the employee's fault? Of course. But it was also the business owner's fault for not respecting the schedule and the structure it provided.

Had I been the owner, and had my employee been that late without cause (a trip to the hospital; a car breakdown outside of cell phone range), I might have fired the employee on the spot. If the employee was particularly good, I might have issued a warning, and fired the employee the second time the employee was hours late. But I certainly wouldn't have waited a year. A year meant that the schedule had no meaning. Ignoring the problem gave the employee tacit permission to misbehave.

Another local business fired one of its three managers for failing to follow a different schedule. The manager would occasionally skip the night deposit, taking care of the deposit the next time the manager drove past the bank. Which meant that the books for the business were off considerably. It also meant that the manager had

Time Management

an entire day's receipts just riding around in the car. The manager was a nice person, without guile. It was just a case of being clueless. In this instance, the manager was clueless exactly twice: the first time, the manager got a warning; the second time, the manager got fired.

Schedules are schedules are schedules.

So...

You work for yourself. Why do you need a schedule?

You need a schedule to help you manage your time, to acquire discipline, and to meet deadlines. Once you become adept at your business, you will know how many hours something will take. You'll be able to schedule your time very well. You'll know *in advance* when you're overextended or underextended. You'll know when you have to work extra hard and when you have some leisure time. You'll know when you need to hire help, even in the short term.

You'll also be able to compare your schedule with that of the people you do business with and come up with a joint schedule that suits you both. That's what I did with the publishing house that gave me its internal schedule, and what I tried to do with the start-up I had to leave. Because I'm very scheduled and I've been doing this a long time, I knew that my March, April, and May would be crammed. (They were.) I also knew that I needed to work extra hard in June, July, and August because I'd lose two, maybe three weeks of work in September due to two trips (and all the planning that goes into such trips). I also knew I'd be tired when I returned, so I'd have to schedule lightly.

What level of schedule do you need? That's determined by your business. Most businesses need some kind of external schedule, marked by deadlines and contracts. But most employees—including you—need an internal schedule.

Just because a retail store is open from 10 to 5 doesn't mean the owner should spend the entire time behind the counter twiddling her thumbs as she waits for customers. She needs to have a schedule to change the inventory, to make bank deposits, to clean the store itself. She might put inventory up on eBay, which has its own scheduling demands, and she might have external deadlines imposed by the state and municipality in the form of tax documents. Even something with a seeming simple schedule might be a lot more complex when viewed from the inside.

Other businesses work off appointment schedules or on construction schedules. Some have deadlines. Others have seasonal demands. All of them valid. All of them create external schedules.

But external schedules mean nothing if you don't have your internal schedule under control. How do you do that?

You work backwards.

Think of it this way. When you went to your day job, you had a schedule. Let's say you had to be there at nine a.m., and unlike the employee mentioned above, you couldn't be five minutes late without a phone call and a damn good reason.

So you figured the time in your head. You had a thirty-minute commute that could stretch to forty-five on bad days. You had to drop the kids off at school, which was fifteen minutes out of your way.

That meant you had to leave the house no later than eight o'clock. It took you an hour to get ready, counting shower and breakfast. If you lived on your own, you could get up at seven and make it. But you didn't. It always took an extra fifteen minutes to get the kids out of bed. Plus, you always hit the snooze button twice. No matter how hard you tried, you couldn't break yourself of that habit.

So, to be safe, you set your alarm for six in the morning, knowing you had built leeway into your schedule. You could oversleep an hour and still get to work on time. Maybe with practice, or as the kids got older, you could shave a half an hour off of that, and get up at six-thirty. Or maybe you convinced your spouse to take the kids. Then you could get up at seven.

We all make those kinds of decisions, every day. Now you have to make them for your business. Let's say yours is a deadline-oriented business, like mine. The external deadline is in stone. So you don't want to miss it, not even if you get the flu or you lose an employee or your computer dies.

So you move the hard deadline a month earlier or two months earlier, and shoot for the new date. Then you count backwards.

In your backwards count, you must be realistic. Let's go back to the getting-to-work metaphor. A friend of mine once told me he lived ten minutes away from work when there was no traffic. The problem was the commute took thirty minutes when the traffic was going the speed limit. If there was a jam, his commute took an hour. (This was why, he told me later, he decided to walk—he actually got there quicker. But that's a digression about a health decision, as well as a scheduling decision.)

If you worked at top speed, you could probably get the project done in a month. But top speed isn't always possible. In fact, top speed usually leads to mistakes and burnout.

At your slowest speed, barely working at all, you could get the project done in four months. But that would be dull and probably counterproductive, since most of us who work on deadline get paid as the deadlines get met.

So how to find a happy medium?

First, buy a calendar. Write in holidays, days off, and vacation days. If you have chronic health problems, like I do, plan for those as well. (I usually plan for an unscheduled week off somewhere in a quarterly schedule.) Put in personal time, like parent-teacher conferences, the kids' soccer matches, dinner and a date with your spouse. Those days are days away from work.

Then figure you can finish the project in 75 days of steady work (add the one month at top speed to the four months of slow speed and divide by two. That gives you 2.5 months or 75 days). Count backwards from your early deadline, skipping the days off and half days. Circle that date on your calendar. That's your drop-dead start date. Do not miss it. You might finish the project earlier than your early deadline. Good for you. You've just become reliable.

But you might have to struggle to meet your early deadline because—guess what? Life happens. If you're struggling, you have some time built into your schedule. But your drop-dead deadline is just that. Something you cannot miss.

Play whatever mind games it takes to make your schedule work. And *write it all down*. The early deadline, the start date, the time you think it will take to finish.

Because you might have to juggle everything if another deadline gets into the mix.

This happened to me in April. I agreed to write a story that would take quite a bit of research. The editor implied that the story would be due in June. When I asked for his actual deadline, he gave me May 15. I looked at that, looked at my already-crammed schedule, and realized that I would have to work late into the night to get it done. But I could do it, research and all. It meant that I had to shave some things out of my schedule—mostly following the news, which I do obsessively. No morning newspaper. No evening newscasts. No peeking at news websites. I took to listening to NPR on my iPhone because the app let me download and listen in the middle of the night if need be, or when I was taking out the garbage or feeding the cats.

I adjusted a few other deadlines closer to their drop-deads than I liked. And I didn't write ahead on the *Freelancer's Guide*, for instance, although I planned to. But I managed to make it work. I got it all done, and done well.

I would have had to turn the editor down, though, if I hadn't already had extra time built into my schedule. And I would have lost some significant revenue.

Do what it takes to set up your internal schedule. I use calendars and computerized reminders. I also maintain a daily, weekly, and monthly to-do list. I frequently look ahead at my list, so that I make sure I'm on track.

I work on a project basis—sometimes working 12-hour days, sometimes working 6-hour days. (Occasionally slacking with 4-hour days). Others work on an hourly schedule. They sit at their desks from 9 to 5 just like they would if they had a day job. Or they give themselves a certain number of tasks to complete each hour.

Time Management

That minute level of scheduling is an individual thing. But there are two things that must be absolute:

1. Your schedule must help you complete work.

That sounds so elementary. But if I had an hourly schedule, I'd subvert it and get nothing done. I learned that a long time ago. However, I love to finish things, so I try to finish as many projects as possible in the space of a year. I also like to challenge myself, so I make sure most of the projects are outside my comfort zone.

Long ago, I defined the things I could not cut from my schedule. An hour for meals. (Half an hour for lunch, if need be.) Reading. Exercise. A good night's sleep. An hour of TV per night. I could jettison those things, but not for long. Those were absolutes. And if I skipped some, like exercise and sleep, I wouldn't be effective at my job. So there are times I eat at my desk, but I skip an hour of TV before I skip my daily run. (Dammit.) You have things like that, too. Be honest about them. That'll help you keep your schedule and meet your deadlines.

2. You must enforce your schedule.

Just like that business owner who let his employee arrive late every day for a year (!), you risk losing control of your business if you think of a schedule as a suggestion rather than something written in stone. You'll run from crisis to crisis like that publisher I mentioned, instead of completing good and productive work on time.

Not to mention the fact that if you use a schedule as a suggestion instead of a structure, you'll be in a constant state of panic. Everyone from your suppliers to your creditors to your clients will be angry with you for neglecting one or another detail. Your business will suffer, even if you thrive on conflict. And, ultimately, you'll end up hating the job you created for yourself.

A schedule is as essential to a business as the skeleton is to the human body. Often outsiders can't see the schedule—or just get hints of it—but they'd know if it were missing. A human being would be a packet of flesh and fluids without the skeleton. A business is just a bunch of good intentions without the structure provided by a schedule.

Figure out your schedule—both internal and external. Refine it as time goes on. Figure out what works for you and what doesn't. Then implement it. Make sure that the people around you know about the schedule *and respect it*. You have to respect it, as well. It's the thing that will make or break your business.

Why do you think I hadn't missed in seventy-one weeks of the *Freelancer's Guide? Schedule*, my friends. Some weeks, it was the only thing that got me to the computer—despite being tired or cranky or just plain reluctant. It got me to the computer tonight, even though I would much rather be working on a new project that has me all excited or reading those five new pre-ordered books.

I have time for both of those things in my schedule. And I can get to them now, since this week's work is done.

Deadlines

Here's the problem with waiting until the last minute to do something: the day arrives and it is the worst possible day to do that thing. Take today, for example. I have a migraine, I didn't sleep much, it's the hottest day of the year so far, and we're moving. In fact, we slated today to do a lot of the major moving, so I've been picking, lifting, walking, and cleaning for the past six hours with only one break for dinner, which I *inhaled*.

I'm still cleaning—as I write this, the washing machine is humming and so is the dishwasher (with its third load)—because once you move something from Point A to Point B, you realize just how dirty Point A has gotten and how you couldn't stomach putting that thing away in Point B until the thing is clean. So there will be more picking, lifting, walking and cleaning tomorrow, but at least tomorrow, I don't have to end the day writing this.

If I fall asleep while writing this…well, you'll never know except that the Gone Fishing notice will be on the website tomorrow. The greater danger is that my brain will shut off, which it does with an audible clunk (at least, it's audible to me). Then you will notice, because my aphasia will kick in and while I'll have perfectly spelled words in this piece, they won't be the right ones in the right order.

Normally, I work ahead of the deadline. I thought of doing that this week, considering we had the move today, but I figured I wouldn't need to do so. I hadn't counted on six-plus hours, a migraine, and heat. (Well, to the rest of you: warmth. It rarely gets above 70 here, and today it did. So for us, that's hot. For most of you in August, that's cool.) I didn't plan as well as usual.

I have had a couple of deadline issues this week. Writing isn't a science—if it were, every publishing company would only publish bestsellers. I always plan to revise or redraft (write new from scratch) whenever I turn in an assigned piece. So I try to turn in those pieces early just in case something goes wrong.

This past week, my strategy paid off. I turned in a story that the editor hated. It's a damn fine story, but oh, did it miss the anthology's mark. It's already in the mail elsewhere. But now, I have to write an entirely new, more suitable story for that anthology. If I had pushed the deadline like I have with this column, I would have missed out entirely. I wouldn't get my second (or third) chance at the anthology.

Instead, I turned in my story two months early—three if you figure that most editors build in a month's lag time for those silly writers who are always late. I will get my second chance.

There are other benefits to meeting a deadline early. One of my writer friends turned in her second series novel on time. Some other writer missed a deadline, so my friend's novel has been moved on the publishing schedule to a much better publication date.

Another benefit? More work. Often, I get extra work because I write well fast (some writers don't) and I meet deadlines. So remember those writers I mentioned who are always late? If one of them misses a short story deadline, and the anthology editor still needs to fill space, he calls me. Sometimes I will have two and three stories in an anthology under various (and occasionally secret) pen names, mostly because other writers can't seem to get off their butts.

(Which might be a problem for me tonight, as well, considering how my muscles have started seizing up.)

So, since I'm thinking about deadlines, let's take a look at them and how they apply to all freelancers.

Time Management

In some professions, deadlines are easy. In retail, the only deadlines that happen every day are your opening and closing times. It's important to hold fast to those times, because you'll lose customers who get disgusted when you're not open at 10 a.m. (like you said you'd be) or have closed two hours early because you got bored. That's the quickest way to kill a retail business.

The other deadlines in retail don't apply to all shops. If you celebrate the holidays, then you need to get your holiday merchandise out by a particular date. (As I write this, the "holiday" is back to school and all the shops are stocked with notebooks and pens and backpacks and gadgets that didn't even exist when I was in school. There will be a short breather (very short) and then the Halloween stuff will appear, and I will have to guard my pocketbook, because I tend to buy little ghostie and vampiry doodads by the dozens (and I don't want to move them from one place to another).)

Book retailers have to place new books out on the publication date, not before, and not after. Some books get embargoed, meaning the bookseller isn't even supposed to open the box until the day of publication. But those are usually highly anticipated books, and who can blame the bookseller for taking a peek for his own personal reading pleasure? Certainly not me.

But for the most part, the deadlines in retail are the same deadlines that other businesses have: paying the bills, the employees, and the taxes on time. Otherwise, if you own your own shop, you work in a relatively deadline-free environment.

I can't think of many other professions that can claim that. Of course, many of those professions have a different name for the deadline. Doctors and dentists have appointment schedules. Deadlines don't come into play unless treatment needs proper timing.

Lawyers also have appointment schedules, but they also have real deadlines, particularly if they are trial lawyers. The court sets the deadlines and a lawyer misses them at his (and his client's) peril. That's why trial lawyers can disappear from their daily life for months at a time, as they prepare witnesses, go over evidence, and plan strategy for the really big trial. And many lawyers don't sleep much during that time either, because the lawyer has to be in his chair when court begins in the morning or he faces punishment from the judge for delaying everyone else.

A lot of professions have non-performance penalties. If you're a tax accountant and you miss filing deadlines, you can get fined. Contractors have time-overruns built into their bids, but if they go too far over, they risk fines or penalties or loss of revenue from the client.

Some professions are constrained by time on both ends. A contractor can't work 24/7 on a project, like Dean did on one writing deadline. The law doesn't allow it, for one thing (most towns have ordinances prohibiting noise during the hours between 11 p.m. and 7 a.m.) and generally speaking, the client wouldn't like it either. Not to mention the union regulations and the labor law restrictions on many folks who own their own businesses.

So when contractors bid on a project, they have to know reasonably well how much time that project will take. The deadlines matter for the client—so the client knows when he'll have use of his kitchen again, for example—and for the contractor. The contractor doesn't have just one client. He'll want to bid on other jobs that will follow this one. Let me tell you from experience, there's nothing more annoying than a contractor who can't get to your job because he hasn't finished the previous job yet.

Some professions, like mine, allow you to complete the job early. Those professions are like mine in more ways than one: our work is generally subjective. Architects deal with this. One wag, writing about New York City, mentioned that in New York, large projects have a pattern: The idealistic project, the sacrificial project, the realistic project, and the actual project. The idealistic project, he said, is the one that gets the ball rolling—the one that allows property to change hands, and the city government to change the ordinances. The sacrificial project is the one everyone likes, but is impractical. It might actually get underway, but gets stalled by lawsuits from former landowners or neighbors who hate the idea of anything going into that neighborhood. The realistic project is, then, the compromise between the first two—the one that the lawsuits settle on, the one that fits the land use designs. The realistic project is often so ugly that someone decides to hire one more architect to get one more design. And that design is always the actual project, because by then, everyone is tired of the process and ready to move on to something else.

If the job is small enough, the same architect works on all four projects (and expects the pattern). If it's large enough, the job might provide work for two generations of architects over the lifetime of the project. All of those architects, however, meet deadlines, set by the client or the city or both. The project itself will then have deadlines and so will the court cases.

Deadlines are, no matter what your profession, a fact of life.

So then, why do so many people miss those deadlines?

I'm not the person to ask. If you'll look at the next section on discipline, you'll see that I've been meeting deadlines since I was in broadcasting. (Hell, I met them before that—I was one of the annoying kids who got my homework done early.)

Everyone eventually will miss a deadline. Life intrudes. Illness strikes, emergencies happen. A friend who had a strict deadline got seriously injured at a work-related event and that injury turned into a life-threatening series of complications. So instead of meeting her deadline early, my friend was two months late. Had she waited until the last minute to start, however, she would have been six to eight months late. The fact she could work at all with all of the health problems was a miracle in and of itself.

What do you do if you're going to be late? You inform the client the instant that you know. No excuses. You explain the reason for the tardiness and apologize. Sincerely. Then you set a new deadline.

If you're in a profession where no new deadline is possible (the judge refuses to change the court date, for example), you come up with another solution. You might have to give up the job and give it to someone else who is as (or more) qualified than you are.

But the bottom line is simple: you keep your client informed of your progress. You never ever disappear or go dark. You never miss the deadline and then apologize. You tell your client what the problem is, and what your solution will be. If you turn out to be wrong—if you're able to meet the original deadline—do so. If you overestimated how quickly the problem would end, tell the client the moment you know and change the deadline again. Offer a refund. Offer to find someone to replace you. Generally, the client will refuse because the client wants you for the job. But sometimes the client has needs you don't even know about, and the client can't wait for you. Nor should he have to.

Accept that missed deadlines happen and plan for them. If you have the kind of business that takes half the payment at the beginning of the project and half on completion, realize that you might have to repay that first payment if you miss the deadline. (Or repay a percentage of it.) Try not to spend that payment before the job is done.

(This is why so many professions separate costs out by time. You pay by the hour, with a retainer up front. Or you pay expenses *and* the cost of the job. Expenses happen no matter what. The cost of the job might have to be repaid if the deadline doesn't get met.)

I've mentioned deadlines in previous sections. I've stressed how important they are, and I'm sure you've nodded, agreeing with me, knowing that I'm right, the way your teacher is right when she wants the assignment on time.

But deadlines are more complicated than that. Because in the real world, deadlines add up to only one thing: Your reputation. If you meet your deadlines, you have a good reputation. If you're early, you have a sterling reputation. If you're chronically late no matter how good your actual work is, you'll have a bad reputation.

A freelancer with a bad reputation eventually becomes someone else's employee. In other words, a bad reputation will cost you your business. And the quickest way to ruin your own reputation is to consistently miss your deadlines.

I'm a few sentences away from meeting my deadline tonight. Self-imposed, yes. But worthwhile all the same. In some ways, I see

Time Management

these posts as an appointment with those of you who visit every week. Some of you visit as soon as I post and some of you struggle in throughout the week. But you know I'll have something new on the site when you click to it.

That matters to me. It matters enough that I'm sitting in my office to the music of the dishwasher and washing machine (and now, the dryer) as I play Bach loud enough to wake the dead—or at least to keep me awake as I type this.

Keep your deadlines. Be on time for your appointments. Open your stores on time and don't close them early. Respect your clients. Then, they'll respect you in return.

Discipline

I don't want to write this post. I have half a dozen reasons—some of them very good—as to why. First, my chronic illness has flared this week, so I'm struggling against my health. Second, Thursday is one of my annual days off, and I usually post the Guide on Thursday. If I were working a regular job, this day off would be on my calendar—and would have been since before I was hired. Third, I am moving my office and it looks like this week is D-Day for the desk, computer, printer, and calendar, the very things I use to write 95% of the time.

Those are the good reasons. Here are the whiney reasons: First, my office cat died two weeks ago. I really don't like going into my office when she's not there. Second, I gave up my nonfiction career for a reason twenty-three years ago. I don't like writing nonfiction. It's work. Fiction, on the other hand, is fun. Third, I've been doing this *Guide* for a while now and it's no longer new (or as my husband would say, it's not bright and shiny), so it's become a chore—something with a deadline that must be met, instead of something I look forward to doing.

I might admit the whiney reasons to friends. But here are the final reasons, the ones that come up when I'm tired and not feeling well, like today. First, I'd rather be reading. (Honestly, I'd always rather be reading.) Second, I want cake. (That's Thursday.) Third, I want to watch the news. And get e-mail. And go on Twitter. And surf the net. And, and, and....

I don't want to be sitting in my empty office, groggy from a nap that only left me feeling marginally better, writing part of a book that isn't under contract and might never be.

So why am I here?

Because I anticipated this day. Seriously. I knew this day was coming. And I planned for it.

Here's why I'm sitting in my empty office, groggy from a nap that left me feeling only marginally better, writing part of a book that isn't under contract.

You.

I have met my deadline on the *Freelancer's Guide* every week since April 2nd. I post, you make comments and e-mail me. Some of you have donated to the *Guide*, and some of you have subscribed, so I have a very real obligation to hit the mark, week after week, until this project is done.

That's the main reason. In fact, that's the only reason I'm here this week.

That reason negates all the complaints I had in the first paragraph.

But the complaints in the second—the ones I call the whiney reasons—have come up before. And despite the fact that two of them sound project-specific, they're not. They come up, with different rationales, with every single project I work on.

I would always rather start a new project than work through the middle of another project. And the *Freelancer's Guide* is in the muddy middle. How far into the middle, I can't tell you. I can never estimate easily how much material I have left.

Besides, I love beginnings. Not the actual moment of work, which can be hard as I try to figure out how to approach the project, but grooming the idea and preparing it for the actual writing. That bright and shiny part of writing is appealing to me, and I always

Time Management

have more than one project going just to keep that bright and shiny part of my brain occupied.

I work well at the end of a project as well. Gone are the days when I'd just skip the end (I got tired of Dean looking at me and saying, "You skipped the last 10,000 words *again*"). When I know how something will end, I want it finished, and I work harder to get it done so that I can move onto the bright and shiny new thing.

Then there's the daily battle against "I want to read" and "I want to eat" and "I want to see a movie/news/TV." The battle against "I want to be doing something else, something that sounds fun, because right now, this project isn't fun."

Or as I usually say to someone who complains on television (and dammit, they can't hear me), "Wah."

Discipline gets a freelancer past all the complaints, but it's not the discipline you imagine from all those movies about military school or from watching Tiger Woods' (pre-divorce) interviews about his dogged determination to be the first on the course and the last to leave.

Discipline gets the job done, as Malcolm Gladwell noted in his controversial book, *Outliers*. The musicians who put in more practice hours have more success than those who put in fewer hours. Same with athletes, and same with writers and almost everyone else in the arts. Both Bill Clinton and Barack Obama spent more time on the campaign trail in their initial successful Presidential bid than any of their opponents did—both in hours per day, and days per week.

But *how* did they do that? How do some musicians, playing the same instrument with the same intensity as other musicians, manage to hit the practice room more often? Why does Tiger Woods work harder than *every other professional golfer* on the course —especially since he says, quite frankly, that it's the hours of practice that make him the golfer he is.

Let's stick with Tiger for a moment. My husband used to be a professional golfer, so golf is important to our household, and Dean has more insight than most about the sport. We've watched Tiger since he won the U.S. Amateur competition in the 1990s. Dean told me then that this kid would be a phenom, and he is.

More than a decade later, Tiger Woods can rest on his laurels, but he doesn't. He won the U.S. Open in 2008, playing for four days with a destroyed knee and a cracked bone. Golf days last six hours or so, and golf, for those of you who don't play or follow the sport, hurts knees more than any other part of the body because of an unnatural twisting motion that the golfer must make when he swings.

It takes discipline to go to that course every day, in extreme pain, but you see it not just in Tiger Woods, but in most athletes at the pro level. It's so bad in most professional sports that teams have doctors on stand-by to order a badly injured player off the court/field so that the injury will not become permanent and career-ending.

What causes this attitude? Sportscasters call that "heart," but it's more than heart. We've all seen high school players with heart, players who will give their all when the time comes to win the big game.

But it's not the big game that matters. It's the practice. It's sitting down to play scales for the 50,000th time because you need to warm up your hands before getting to Mozart. It's the drudgery of the same thing every day, with no defined ending.

It's the ability to overcome the urge to grab the bright and shiny and interesting to finish what you've started.

It's—and I'm sorry to say this, folks—it's what gets you to your day job five days per week, fifty-two weeks per year.

The problem is that most people don't apply that same discipline to their freelance work. There are reasons for this, which I'll get to. And, before the comments come in, let me add that I do realize that most people at a day job are not working at their best. Maybe they never do as well as they could. Many never reach their full potential. Most don't even try.

So what is it that makes some people work hard at their free-

Time Management

lance careers while others work hard enough to get by or can't figure out a way to work at all?

It's not discipline. It's figuring out how to get yourself to work. Seriously. What gets most people to their day jobs isn't the job. It's the money they get from the job, money that lets them pay the bills and support their family. Sure, a handful *like* their work, but most like the paycheck and benefits better.

Here's the problem: there are no paychecks and benefits when you work for yourself. If that's your motivation for working, then you're not going to have much luck freelancing—providing you carry that motivation into your freelance work.

Let's boil it down a bit more. When you begin freelancing, you do it for the love. Often you wait for the muse or until you get an order or if a friend asks for your help with something that you're good at. Eventually, you make some money at this, and then you realize you might be able to make a living at it.

Already, bad habits have formed. You start doing this as a hobby, *after* everything else of importance gets finished. It feels natural to do the freelance work last.

Other things are always important. Your daughter skins her knee, the phone rings, a friend needs help moving. You have to learn to make your hobby or the thing you did only when you "had time" become your first priority.

How do you do that?

Unfortunately, I can't tell you. What you need to do is specific to you. There is no magic bullet, no one-size-fits-all answer.

But let me give you some ideas, based on my own experience.

And as I typed those words, I heard my writing friends giggle. They are all convinced that I'm the most disciplined person they know. They're wrong. In most things, I lack discipline entirely.

Unlike most of my writing friends, I have not held a full-time job for years. Why? Discipline. At some point, the paycheck isn't enough for me. I hate having someone tell me what to do, and that always triumphs.

Even the radio job, which I loved, didn't last long. I quit four separate times. Each time the station hired me to be *interim* news director at my insistence. I didn't want the permanent job. So I stayed until someone new came on board, and came back as interim director when that someone new left. I remained at the station in between *as a volunteer*, working a few nights per week. But I didn't want to be an employee there. The only thing that broke that years-long cycle, by the way, was my move out of town.

Discipline has always been a major issue for me. I get bored easily, and I don't play well with others. So hiring a personal trainer, for example, would never work for me. I would do my best to circumvent anything the trainer told me.

In my forties, I had a piano teacher. I stayed until I learned how to play the instrument adequately. Then I realized I was seeing how much practice it actually took to convince the teacher I had spent days at it instead of an hour or two. Once I fooled her a few times, we were done.

This is why I never became a musician. I didn't have the discipline. And I love music. At one point in my life, I played 15 different instruments. (Only two of them really well.) I just don't love music enough to conquer my discipline problem.

I love writing enough to work through each issue as it comes up. How? By figuring out what stopped me from getting a day's worth of work done involved.

Each time I solved one issue, another cropped up. Then I would have to solve that one. This pattern continues to this day.

When I discuss this with students, I tell them that gaining discipline is a series of mind games. Your mind will find good and effective ways to stop you. You have to figure out ways around them. The old cliché about when a door closes go through a window applies here.

I can sense the frustration among you now. I'm not being specific enough to help. So let's go back through my initial points, above, and I'll tell you how I get around them. Maybe that will strike a chord.

First, health issues. I'll deal with this more in the illness section below. But in short, here's what helps me. I imagine making my excuses to a boss. If a good boss would let me go home sick or encourage me to stay away from the office, then I stay away from the computer. But if I can put in a day of so-so work, I do. I store up projects for days when my illness is present, but not so bad that I have to spend the day in bed. Those are the projects I do when I'm not feeling well.

Second, my annual days off. I have a few of them—birthday, anniversary, Christmas, and a couple of others. If I don't take those days, I'm angry at myself. Sometimes I take an entire week around it. That's just reasonable for any job. There's more on this in the section about vacations below.

Third, moving my office. I haven't done that for years. It's a good excuse not to work, except that I have deadlines, just like you would at a day job. I had to figure out a way to work while I'm in the middle of this transition. Because if it's not this transition, it's another transition. Life is full of them, and you have to figure out how to put in your freelance hours, even while everything changes around you.

But those are bigger events. It's the small ones that interfere with discipline. Let's address what I call the whiney complaints.

First, I would rather read. It took me an entire summer to figure out that reading, for me, will suck all my time out of every single day. I cannot start a book with breakfast or I will read until I go to bed.

How did I discover this? I had a day job that went part-time. I opted to take the afternoons off. When the job had been full-time, I read during my lunch break. So I continued this habit on the part-time schedule—and got nothing done.

I tried "disciplining" myself. I would put the book down and try to go to work, only to find myself reading again. "Disciplining" —forcing myself to quit—didn't work. No matter how hard I tried, I simply could not stop reading, even when I finished the book. I'd move to the next one.

So the key for me wasn't *quitting* reading. It was *not starting*. I set the books aside until I got x-amount of work done each day.

This isn't easy. It required actual hiding of the books. I enlisted my then-husband's help, making sure the books were out of sight.

Eventually, I learned that I worked hard and fast if I knew I could read when I was done. I got my work done, and then I read. Problem solved.

It sounds so easy, but it took months of trial and error. No amount of "forcing" myself got me to change my habits. I had to figure out where the problem started, and nip it in the bud.

Second, I want cake. (Don't we all?) That's usually a sign to me that I'm hungry. I need to figure out if I'm really hungry or—catch this—bored with what I'm doing. If I'm bored, I think I'm hungry, because that's one of the few things I will get up from my desk to deal with. If I need a meal, I eat. But my subconscious loves to trick me (and my hips) by convincing me to leave when I'm not through.

Often, the "I'm hungry" reaction comes when I'm working on something particularly difficult or something I don't want to do. Again, it took many months (and too many calories) to figure this one out. Now, before I get something to eat, I ask myself this: Do I like what I'm working on? If the answer is no, I generally stay at my desk.

Note that I do not ask myself if I'm hungry. I've already identified hungry, and the answer would be yes. But I figured out that my subconscious has learned a mind game to convince me to get away from the computer, one that makes me think I'm hungry (or craving food, like cake) and gets me to leave *when I don't need to*.

We all have mind games like this, and they're hard to identify. The question should always be: Is work going well? Because if it is, and I'm hungry, I have trouble tearing myself away. If it isn't, I'll make up any damn reason to leave my desk.

Third, I want to watch the news, download e-mail, look at the Internet, do Twitter....in other words, do something else entirely.

This was almost as bad for me as reading was. I learned to keep my office spare. My computer has Internet access and it also has e-mail access. I have shut those programs down. I've tossed away all games that were initially on my computer. There is no phone or television in my office. I have a stereo and a radio tuned to a classical channel. No news of any kind allowed here.

Why? Because they all distract me. Rather than "discipline" myself to overcome the temptation, I remove the temptation entirely. In order to download my e-mail, I have to go to a different computer, one with an existing e-mail program, and download from there. I need to go to a different room to watch television. I can't even hear the phone ring in my office.

These were all tough things to learn. The Internet is particularly sneaky because you feel like you're working when you're online. You are not working—even if, like me, a small part of your business comes through the Internet. You're not doing your core business. I have a number of writing friends who refuse to remove the Internet from their computer. Those friends get very little done. All of them have spouses who work, and so the writer doesn't have to bring in a lot of money. All of them frown at me when I suggest removing the Internet from their writing computer.

Everyone has these leaks, as the poker players call it. A leak is something that drains your income, something that has nothing to do with your work. And it's often something you're not willing to give up.

You have to learn how to control this leak and make it work for you. And here's the tough part: If you can't control it, seek help. I went into therapy a number of years ago to help with one of my writing issues, something that got in the way of my business. And as much as I hate authority, I listened to that counselor, because being a successful writer meant more to me than the leak.

However, had we worked on my discipline issues with music, I probably would have blown off the therapy within weeks. I have never had the discipline there, and I really don't want it. Not deep down.

And that's the final issue. If you want a successful freelance career of any kind, you'll overcome the things that get in your way.

You can't do it all at once. You have to tackle one problem at a time. But you're willing to work on those problems.

If you're not willing to solve the problem after years of trying, then you probably don't want this freelance career (whatever it is) as much as you think you do.

Discipline is not about forcing yourself to improve. It's about wanting to get better.

That's the difference between Tiger Woods and all those other golfers. Tiger wants to be the best, and he knows the only way to do that is to work harder than everyone else. But he doesn't define himself as the best *right now*. He means *the best ever*. He keeps Jack Nicklaus's stats on his wall, trying to beat them. Tiger's not playing the current field. He's playing the entire field from the dawn of recorded golf history.

And he's doing a good job at knocking down the records.

But here's the key. He's not doing this for his fans. He's not doing it for his (late) father or for golf history. He's doing it for himself. Because he wants to. Because that's his goal.

So...

How do you get disciplined?

Here are a few thoughts.

1. Define what you want to achieve.

Not other people's goals for you. Not what your parents want or your spouse wants. What do you want? And how badly to do you want it? Will you die disappointed if you don't achieve it? Will you feel like a failure? Or will you shrug and move on to the next thing?

2. Make a list of the things that get in the way of that achievement.

If everything you list comes from the outside, then you have another problem. For example, writers often say they can't get published because the publishing industry is impossible to crack or they need an agent or they can't figure out how to submit their work. Those, my friends, are excuses. Other people have succeeded in your industry. Figure out how they did it, and then try it yourself.

By "what gets in the way," I mean what part of *you* gets in the way. What are you doing to block your success? How do you change that? Sometimes the change is minor, like asking yourself whether you are really hungry or avoiding work. Sometimes the change is major, like the one thing I mentioned (deliberately vaguely) that forced me to go to therapy. I couldn't change that one on my own—but it was *my* problem, and I had to find a solution. I just needed help doing so.

3. Change your thought patterns.

When you decide to go full-time freelance, realize that your hobby has just become your job. That realization alone will take time. Then figure out how to make your freelance work a priority in your own mind. Apply patterns from your day job to your freelance work.

Ask these questions:

What made you go to your day job every morning?

What made you stay there?

What made you work on days when you felt crummy?

What made you work on days when you had somewhere better to go?

And so on. Use those answers to design your freelance work.

For example, Dean works hard when he's under deadline. He has trouble working when he has no deadlines at all. The key for him is to create deadlines—or to get someone from the outside (an editor, usually) to give him a deadline.

I didn't think I had that issue until I started the *Freelancer's Guide*. Then I realized that I never finish nonfiction unless I have a deadline. I don't like writing nonfiction. I love writing fiction and will do it without a deadline. But the deadline gets me to finish nonfiction projects—my two columns, some articles, and now this.

By meeting my deadline on this *Guide* every week, I've also established something else. I've got a streak going. I hate breaking streaks, so that's motivation to work on weeks like this one, when I could just as easily post a note that the *Guide* is on a one-week hiatus.

I learned long ago that I have to love what I'm doing to sustain the work. I loved working at the radio station, but hated it when I was in charge. So I kept quitting the paying work to go back to volunteering.

I love writing fiction, so I continue to do it, even when times are tough.

When I need to be disciplined, I have to find the love at the center of what I'm doing. Here's an example. I have tried to maintain a regular exercise program since the middle-aged spread hit in my mid-thirties (thanks in part to that hunger thing, above).

I started with an exercise I love, swimming. But it was inconvenient. I had to drive half an hour each way to the pool. The hours were irregular, and I'd often lose too much work time. So I started riding my bicycle. I enlisted the help of a friend from the gym. I had to meet her a designated time every day. That got me out of the house.

We couldn't sustain the rides. Then I fell off the bike and broke my arm, the second serious bike accident in my life. (The first, when I was nine, smashed my face so badly, I still have occasional dental surgeries to repair the damage.) I realized that cycling on the Oregon Coast along a highway with no bike lanes (there are none for more than 100 miles) is too dangerous for me.

So I decided to run. When I made this decision, I couldn't run for a minute without feeling ill. I didn't like it. I had never liked running. Worse, I got bored quickly.

But I love music. If a song that I like comes on the radio, I crank the volume. If I'm alone in the house, I dance. So I put my favorite

CDs on my iPod, and promised myself I could run for the length of one song.

I couldn't, not for weeks. Eventually I managed. But I wasn't running because I liked running. I was using that time as an excuse to listen to my favorite music all by myself.

Two years later, I can run for 30 minutes straight. When I feel like it's time to find a new form of exercise, I realize it's time to change the music in my iPod. I'm bored with what's there. I would rather swim, honestly. I would like to be on my bike. But running works for me now. And I've become so conditioned to it that last week, when my iPod battery died, I played some music in my head and finished the workout.

Could I do that every time? Hell, no. But I know how to make myself go out for a daily run now—and how to enjoy it. Set the iPod on shuffle and see what songs come up.

It took me fifteen years to find a form of exercise I can do every day, rain or shine, one that I *will* do. And what gets me out there now isn't the exercise or the need for it.

It's the half an hour of music. Which I love.

So the most important aspect of discipline isn't discipline at all. It's this:

4. Find the love.

Find what you love about what you do, and channel that each and every day. Acknowledge it too. When I finish a run, I check in with myself. Inevitably, I feel better when I quit than I did when I started. I've told Dean that, and sometimes he's gotten me outside by reminding me of it. (I have to tell you, it sometimes pisses me off that I feel better *after* a run when I felt so crummy before the run.) Celebrate your achievement, even if that achievement is just getting to your desk.

Celebrate with something you enjoy.

I used to celebrate a day's writing by reading. Then I started editing, and reading ceased to be a reward for several years. In those years, I celebrated with a good movie or a guilty-pleasure TV show. Now I'm back to celebrating with reading.

Which is what I'm going to do now.

Oh, by the way, I'm no longer groggy from the nap, although I still feel under par. I did run today, and felt better afterwards (dammit!). And I got this section of the *Guide* done, two days early. I'll post it late tomorrow, which will be one day early. Then I'll get my day off. With cake.

That's my reward, along with all the fun things planned for that day.

And that was more than enough to get me into my chair today—even though I didn't want to be here.

Illness

How do you know when you're too sick to work? Seems easy enough to figure out, right? We're all adults. We know when we're sick. But for freelancers, that's a tougher question than it seems.

We all get sick. The serious things—pneumonia, bronchitis, certain types of flu—leave us too ill to get out of bed. They're not the problem to the freelancer. The milder illnesses are.

When you work for someone else, it's easy to know when to go into work. If you had one of those cushy jobs with paid sick leave and paid vacation, chances are you took more sick days than you needed. If you were feeling a little off, and you had the paid time coming to you, you took the day and stayed home. Even seasonal allergies might have warranted a little paid "me" time.

If you had a by-the-hour job without those benefits, you took as little time off as possible. At my last waitressing job, the boss actually had rules about when *not* to come to work. (If you're contagious, she'd say, you must stay home.) People who work by the hour usually need the money. They come to work when they can barely walk because they don't dare lose the hours.

Freelancing is closer to the by-the-hour job, but it's not quite the same. When you freelance, you get paid for piecework. In other words, the more things you finish, the more you get paid.

You finish more things if you put in more hours.

Seems obvious, right? But most people aren't used to being their own boss. Most people are too lenient with themselves. They lose entire days to headaches or the sniffles because they're not feeling "up to par." Days, even weeks, go by while the freelancer waits to feel better.

Here's an ugly truth: *When you work at home, you have no colleagues to distract you. You're constantly assessing how you feel, and always coming up short.*

That's right. You'll probably feel worse day to day when you work at home. Some of it is the solitude. Some of it is the lack of exercise. Some of it is the lack of fresh air.

When you go to a job away from home, you have to walk outside and drive somewhere. When I started freelancing, I'd stay in the house for days on end. It took me a while to realize that a walk around the block was often enough to make me feel energetic and healthy.

So…how *do* you know if you're too sick to work?

It's simple. Imagine the toughest boss you ever worked for. Then imagine telling him (and my toughest boss was a man) that you can't come into work today because…and fill in the reason here.

If you can't imagine yourself telling Tough Boss that reason, then you go to work.

It goes like this: Hi, Tough Boss. I can't come to work today because I have a temperature of 102 and I'm heading to the doctor this afternoon.

Fine, good. My old Tough Boss would have let me out for that.

But imagine this one: Hi, Tough Boss. I can't come to work today because I'm feeling sluggish.

Or…

Hi, Tough Boss. I can't come to work today because I didn't get a good night's sleep last night.

Or…

Hi, Tough Boss. I can't come to work today because I'm not thinking as clearly as I usually do.

Time Management

One or two of those with the Tough Boss I'd had (back in 1980—this dude really lives in my memory) and I would've been fired. Fast.

A friend once told me that people who work at corporate jobs aren't productive every moment of every day. They talk to their colleagues on company time. They daydream. They do make-work to look busy. This friend was a corporate manager who estimated that a good 40% of the time, his employees weren't working at their peak.

On the days they came in feeling "sluggish" or "tired," they probably got less done.

When you work for someone else, you get used to days like that. You know you won't get fired (unless you have other problems with job performance). Your employer knew that was part of the deal when he decided to hire employees in his business. Every self-employed person knows that the hardest worker in the company is always the boss.

On those days when you would go into work with a mild cold or allergies, you get what you could done. Sometimes, you got brownie points just for showing up and keeping your desk warm.

I was so used to working for myself that when I got my single full-time job back in 1984, I caused a huge stir in the office. I worked as an editorial assistant in a textbook publishing house. I got my day's assignments and usually finished them within the first hour of my eight-hour shift.

The other editorial assistants pulled me aside after a week of that and told me to slow down because I was making them look bad. I didn't get it. I figured I was there to *work*, so I worked. I could have done the work of all the editorial assistants and filled up my day. But that wasn't the corporate structure. So I did my hour's worth of work, and spent the remaining seven hours reading the books the company published. My boss promised to promote me if someone in editorial quit. Which no one had for nearly two years. After four months of that, I left the job because I was horribly, unbelievably bored.

(Years later, I got a great part-time job as a secretary for a forensic psychologist. He looked at my résumé and said, "My biggest concern about you is that you're used to working for yourself. I'm hiring you to sit and answer phones. I'm afraid you might get bored." I told him about my experience at the textbook publisher and we both laughed about it. Then he agreed that I could write or read at my desk when he had nothing for me to do. Needless to say, that was the best day job I ever had.)

If you had one of those jobs that let you slack off with regularity, then freelancing is going to be a big shock for you. Unless you modify your behavior right now, you'll be one of those freelancers who gets nothing done for days on end, especially in spring allergy season or when the baby keeps you up all night.

No matter how dedicated you are, the reality is that there will be days when you feel sick, but not sick enough to stay home (from that imaginary Tough Boss). How do you do your best work when that happens?

Well, you don't. You figure out what tasks you can do. I'm writing this piece two days earlier than I planned because today, I'm surviving on Advil and caffeine.

I'm not thinking clearly enough to write fiction. So I'm doing tasks that I find easier than fiction writing. And yes, writing nonfiction is easier than fiction, at least for me. (Besides, I can always clean this essay up later if I don't like what I've done.)

I've been feeling punk for three days now. I've photocopied contracts, put together files for a project that I'm working on with a publisher in Virginia, did research on the next story I'm writing, and cleaned up my office.

I know the pattern of my chronic condition, so I know that in a day or two, I'll be back up to my normal level of energy. Why waste my good days on tasks I can do when I'm not feeling up to par? I'm planning ahead by doing some of this work before it's due.

This is exactly what you would have done at your day job if you were feeling a little under the weather, but you still managed to show up. You'd have done the things you'd been putting off, things that required less effort than your daily tasks.

Just think of Tough Boss. Make your excuses out loud, and see if they'll fly with him. If they won't, then go to your office. Do what you can.

You'll be happy that you did.

Vacations

So last week, we discussed illness and the freelancer. The topic, which also dealt peripherally with taking time off, brought up another time-off question from several readers. Here's it phrased by Jas Marshall:

"When you're a freelancer, how do you take a vacation? When you are your own toughest boss, and you're pushing to produce more stuff so you can get paid, and so on...how do you justify even a single day off when 'I could be editing that novel to get it out the door' or whatever?"

When that question came in, I knew I was in trouble. Because I'm trying to keep this as general as possible about freelancing, not just freelance *writers*. Frankly, freelance writers are a different breed from other freelancers—and, I've been told, I'm a different breed than many freelance writers.

So I opened the question to freelancing friends on four different business e-mail lists that I'm on. The answers are self-selected (meaning this is not a scientific poll), but they're interesting and insightful.

What I asked is this: *A question for the freelancers on the list. When was the last time you took a real vacation?*

I deliberately did not define real vacation, figuring people would do so for me. If their definition wasn't clear from their answers, then I sent a follow-up e-mail, asking how they defined real vacation.

I got some great responses. I couldn't use a few, however, because they came from people who did not freelance at all, but worked at a full-time job for corporations (usually in the arts). They felt slighted. After all, they told me (rather grumpily) not all people with full-time jobs use their vacation time—as I well know. My father never took his vacations nor did he use his sick days as long as he was a professor in the University of Wisconsin system (from 1967-1990; he retired at the age of 75).

But, as Jas's question implies, vacations and time off are tricky for freelancers. A friend of mine, who worked for decades as a freelance therapist, took at least two long vacations per year. She worked out of her garage, remodeled to be a comfortable space with an exterior door, and as a result, she rarely left home. Her work was so emotionally intense that if she didn't take time off on a regular basis, she would have burned out.

Then there's me. When I worked real jobs, I couldn't wait to get home so that I could read, write, and watch TV/movies (create and consume stories, as my husband says). Now I "work" every day at reading, writing, and watching TV/movies. When I travel, I'm storing up experiences for my work—and I'm usually reading and writing along the way.

My last (and only) real vacation came in 2005. I'd had a series of health problems, some serious business setbacks, and some financial reversals. Suddenly, a truckload of money came in, more than expected. Dean and I saved most of it, but we decided to spend a small fraction on a vacation. We meandered all over the West Coast. Our only deadline: tickets to see George Carlin in Las Vegas ten days from the day we left.

We explored, shopped, and saw friends. We bought books. We bought more books. I read books. I did not write. I slept. We visited casinos. Dean played poker. I read—and learned that people look at you strangely when you read books in casinos. We saw many different shows. We saw George Carlin perform what would later become his last HBO special.

It is the first (and only) time I have ever spent more than a week away from writing without going insane. That tells me just how exhausted I was.

Usually, however, I bring my laptop on any trip. I write. I read. I explore. I love visiting cities and seeing their history. But then I return to my hotel room and write about what I've seen. I *enjoy* this, and find it refreshing.

But that's me.

Now, let's hear from other freelancers.

First, the folks who do not make the bulk of their living writing (or editing) fiction:

Shanti Fader's freelance work includes proofreading, copy editing, transcriptions, online research, data entry, and jewelry-making. You can see her jewelry designs at tattedbutterfly.etsy.com.

"If you're talking about vacations taken from freelance work," she writes, "my last vacation was June of 2008, when I took off the week before and after my wedding. I told my regulars I wouldn't be available during those weeks, and didn't actively seek out any other work."

Glenn Hauman, who describes what he does as "whatever needs to be done" at the website comicmix.com writes, "'Vacation' is such a tricky word. There are lots of times I've spent an extra day in a city I had to go to because of a convention. Or in some cases, I'll drive, even though the convention is a good fifteen hours away by car. There are lots of times that I've had to scribble down a thought for later exploitation or take a photo for future reference. So if capturing an inspiration is work or taking the time to develop it out is work, then yeah. There are even vacation moments that turn into work—witness this year's Easter dinner which turned into three hours of tech support for a friend of my mother."

Randy Tatano, who works as a freelance broadcast news reporter, mostly for NBC, writes, "If I can't take vacations, you might as well shoot me. I'd rather cut back in other areas if I have to."

He and his wife generally take one or two trips a year. They just booked a trip to Europe for their 20th anniversary. He has advice for reporters at his blog, tvnewsgrapevine.blogspot.com.

Before Rick Dickson left his job as a liquidation consultant to become a full-time fiction writer, he took only one formal vacation in ten years. He describes his former consulting job like this:

"I was Richard Gere in *Pretty Woman*, except that I was hired by insurance regulators to pull apart dead insurance companies: find the money, prove where it went, and work to get it back. (Mostly profit-sharing, international fronting agreements, and reinsurance contracts.) Sadly, 'no,' I never got the girl."

As to why he took only one formal vacation, he says, "As a consultant, I had a lot of downtime between assignments. When you've got a job where the phone can ring at any time to the question, 'How fast can you be in **insert city name here**?', you need to consider these times to be vacation too. I did a lot of the local things...biking, hiking, flying, and playing tourist. The problem with scheduling a 'real' vacation was that I had to do that months in advance and always ended up needing to postpone due to a big client's emergency call (which meant those vacations never materialized)."

I can empathize. When Dean and I owned and operated our own publishing house, Pulphouse Publishing, we never had a real vacation either, although we traveled all over the United States. In those days before cell phones were cheap and common, we would get off the airplane for a two-hour layover and spend most of that time on a pay phone. We spent a lot of time dashing from place to place, often to meet the needs of the business, and rarely with more than a few hours off.

Vacation time truly does depend on the type of freelancing you do. But most freelancers I know have the problems Rick and Shanti mentioned: Clients who expect the work done *now*. It takes a lot of juggling to get time away—even for your wedding.

Time Management

Freelance writers, editors, and artists have other problems. We used to do this work for free in our time off.

As Gerald M. Weinberg, who has freelanced for more than fifty years, says, "By my definition, a vacation is an escape from work you don't want to do. According to my definition, I've been on a real vacation for a long, long time."

He's been spending his vacation time writing fiction and nonfiction. His most recent book is *Perfect Software And Other Illusions about Testing*. You can find his many, many other publications and fascinating biography at geraldmweinberg.com.

He's not alone in this attitude toward freelancing. I share it. So does Laura Anne Gilman. Laura Anne used to be my book editor at Roc before she saw the light and gave it all up to write her own novels, the most recent being *Blood From Stone*. Check out her very excellent blog at lauraannegilman.net.

About vacations, she writes, "If you want the last time I took a vacation where I did no writing, no editing, nothing related to the day job, I think that was 2004. I was bored."

Dave Wolverton, who has written fifty novels under different names (the latest, *The Wyrmling Horde*), says, "I take a day off every few months, but I'd go nuts if I tried to take two days in a row. I have to be very sick to do that."

Dave keeps two websites in addition to all his other work — runelords.com and davefardland.net.

Some writers aren't as happy about their lack of time off. Russell Davis, whose most recent novel (written as Cliff Ryder) is *The Ties That Bind*, wrote a succinct answer. He took his last real vacation in 1996 and, he editorializes, "that is pretty damn pathetic."

You can find his blog at westernsensibility.blogspot.com.

Some writers just flat out answered my question with dates and times. It amazes me how we can all remember that last "real" vacation—and how, for many of us, it was long ago.

Carole Nelson Douglas, whose most recent novel is *Brimstone Kiss*, writes, "My Last Vacation: February 1987, when my husband

and I drove to Corpus Christi and South Padre Island after moving to Texas in 1984. We had to cut our vacation short and drive back to Fort Worth to get some sales figures my new publisher needed right away for a forthcoming book."

Carole also keeps two websites: carolenelsondouglas.com and dancingwithwerewolves.com.

Laura Resnick's answer was so succinct, I asked her to clarify. To my initial inquiry, Laura wrote, "July 2006." And that was it.

I responded: "No work, no writing at all? What kind of vacation?"

And she answered, "I stopped off in England for two weeks in July 2006, on my way home from Jerusalem. Spent the time visiting friends around the country. However, I did three days of on-site research for a book idea: We drove around, collected brochures, took photos, visited places of particular interest to me viz my short story idea. But I only count *writing* as work; I don't count touring a beautiful area with a particular agenda as work."

For my day-to-day business, as you'll see later, I only count words on the page as work, too. But research is part of writing, and I would have counted Laura's trip as work. To each her own.

Laura, by the way, has written twenty books, including *The Purifying Fire*. She's on the web at LauraResnick.com.

Some writers couldn't remember the exact date of their last vacation. Irene Radford, who writes under various names (her latest novel *Fairy Moon*, was written as P.R. Frost) and blogs at ireneradford.com, initially wrote that she and her husband, Tim, "take day trips when I don't even look for bookstores to do drive-by signings. Other than that? Probably 1993 before I sold my first book."

But then, later e-mails revealed Irene to be in the same category as me, Dave Wolverton, and Laura Anne Gilman. Irene said (and I love this), "Freelancing is as much a calling as a career. I cannot not write. I go insane if I'm not actively creating something in my head or on my computer. More than two days off and I start drifting away from conversations, seeing fictional landscapes instead of actual ones. My fingers itch for pen and paper or the touch of a keyboard."

While Irene wasn't exactly sure when her last vacation was, Keith R.A. DeCandido had to be corrected about the date of his on a public forum. Keith, another one of my editors who gave it all up for the freelance life, answered my question on the board instead of e-mailing me directly. He wrote:

"You mean [a vacation] in which I didn't work *at all?* **thinks** Probably New Orleans in 1997, when I was working for Byron Preiss. For the week prior to the World Fantasy Convention, I did not work and didn't let the office know how to get in touch with me. It was bliss. Every vacation I've taken since has had a work component. (I went full-time freelance in 1998)."

After he posted that, another writer popped on the board with this addition, "Dude, that convention was in 1994," which surprised Keith.

Keith, whom you can find at kradical.livejournal.com, describes his work as "freelance writing (of both fiction and nonfiction) and editing."

His most recent book is *Star Trek: A Singular Destiny*, but his most recent publication would be the ongoing *Farscape* comic books.

Keith's mother, GraceAnne Andreassi DeCandido, also freelances. She describes her work as a freelance writer, editor, and teacher. Her most recent publication is in *The Horn Book* magazine for January/February, 2009. Everything else she does is listed at well.com/user/ladyhawk/gadhome.html.

She writes, "The last real vacation I took was eight glorious days in Paris in 2006. The thing about both freelancing and teaching is that there is almost never a day that I cannot take a couple of hours and do what I want, but at the same time, I am never 'off.' Student e-mail must be answered even late on Saturday night; editing web site material gets done between larger assignments, and I am tied to the academic year tightly since I teach summers too. Those eight days were actually completely free of any work, and it was lovely. But it was a long time ago."

Most writers consider single days away from conventions vacations. The content of Mike Resnick's initial paragraph matches Glenn Hauman's almost exactly:

"Tricky question," Mike writes. "If you mean a day tacked onto the end of a convention, then January of this year. Other than things like that, 1984—we took 10 days in England, and I only spent one day visiting my British editors or doing any kind of business. Didn't do business *during* any of our safaris, but a lot of each turned up in novels and short stories and was always intended to."

Mike writes about six novels per year. His personal website is mikeresnick.com, and that's where you'll find the release dates for his upcoming books.

Michael A. Stackpole, freelance writer, game designer, and creative consultant, gets one vacation per year, a three-day fishing trip in Maine.

"The trick is this," Mike writes. "It's a family outing, and the last two years I'd not have gone if my father didn't need someone to drive him from Vermont to Maine—I would have let work interfere."

Mike, whose latest publication is *The New World*, adds, "Other than that, I really haven't had a vacation in the last 30 years."

You can find out what Mike's been doing for the last 30 years at stormwolf.com (and while you're there, check out his writing newsletter, *The Secrets*).

Jennifer R. Baumer, who hasn't yet succumbed to the temptation of a website, has published over 700 articles in local, regional, and national markets, as well as ghostwritten eight books. She went to Disneyland in March with her husband, but "I worked all through the weekend before and the Monday before we left and had a meeting the day after we returned."

She adds, "It's almost so hard to get ready for a vacation, finishing articles, dealing with deadlines from multiple projects and relaxing clients who panic, that sometimes it feels not worth it.

Conversely, or perhaps exactly the same-ly, it sometimes seems easier and more relaxing to work some during that time than to have it preying on one's mind. (Fiction doesn't count—I wrote fiction both nights we were in the hotel at Disneyland and was perfectly happy.)"

But not all freelance writers have the same attitude toward vacations. Steve Perry, whose latest book is *Predator: Turnabout*, reports that he takes "the camper out once or twice a month for at least a weekend, three days if we can, and at least one longer stint every summer."

Then he adds, "I love my work, but I also want to have a life—what's that old saying? Nobody on their death bed says, 'Gee, I wish I'd spent more time at the office.' If all I did was write, what would be the point?"

You can find many more of Steve's opinions at themanwhonevermissed.blogspot.com (and while there, nag him to write more short stories).

Jane Yolen manages to have a life, as well. She says, "I go to Scotland for four months every year. Have for 18 years. Yes, I still write, but half of every day is playing with friends. And when my kids come to visit, for the 2-4 weeks they are there, we play all day long."

Still, Jane publishes several books a year. This spring alone, three have appeared: *My Uncle Emily*, *A Dragon's Heart*, and *A Mirror to Nature*. You can keep up with her at janeyolen.com.

In her response to my question, Carrie Vaughn, author of the Kitty series, makes her priorities clear: "I've been freelancing since 2007, and I try to take a trip every year. I went to Belize for a week last March (2008) and will be going to Hawaii with my family in June. I also try to take an extra couple of days when traveling for work....I should mention that I love traveling and will take a trip before replacing a broken appliance."

Follow her travels and upcoming publications at carrievaughn.com.

For most freelance writers and editors, however, the biggest factor in taking time off is money.

John Ordover, another of my former editors who has gone freelance, writes, "When freelancing, I was less likely to spend money on a vacation because without a salary coming in, I never knew how long the money in the bank had to last."

John now owns and runs JJO Productions (jjoproductions.com) a media consulting and production company.

Alexandra Honigsberg is even blunter. Alexandra is a freelance writer/editor, an adjunct instructor of Philosophy and Theology at St. John's University, and a freelance lecturer in those fields as well as a freelance musician, a corporate consultant in ethics, and an itinerant priest and chaplain of the Old Catholic Church with an emphasis on interfaith dialogue.

She writes, "I live so close to the bone that any trip is for something that is an absolute necessity and then I tag on a few days before/after for myself and keep a tight budget....I invented the freakin' Stay-cation. I live in NYC...so many fabulous free things to do. I've done all the touristy things in my town and many things off the beaten track as well...a meal in a cool ethnic restaurant can be a mini-vacation, a spa/salon day, a ride up the Hudson on the Dayliner with a picnic lunch, a cheap rental car drive up to Rhinebeck for the day, taking the scenic route...those are affordable ways that I keep my sanity...but no, no real vacations. Just not possible on what I've been making, so far, but hey, I'm still here, still in my great apartment, and still pluggin' away."

Her latest article, "The Un-Ethics of *Watchmen*" can be found on Glenn Hauman's Comic Mix website. Her latest short story, "In His Own Image," appeared in *Ravens in the Library*, edited by Phil Brucato and Sandra Buskirk. She's currently too busy to design a website (clearly!).

Award-winning editor, Ellen Datlow, keeps an eye on the bottom line for the tax man. She writes, "Even when employed, I'd add on days to business trips for vacation. I've rarely gone on trips that are exclusively for pleasure, other than trips with my family for special occasions—my parents' 50th and 60th anniversaries. But since most of my friends are somehow involved in the field, my visits to them are usually tax deductible."

Ellen blogs about her trips and editing at datlow.com. Her latest publication is *Poe*.

One of the friends who often provides the tax deduction for Ellen is Pat Cadigan, who moved from Kansas City to London some years ago. Pat, whose latest short story, "Truth and Bone," can be found in Ellen's *Poe* anthology, "The last time I went on a vacation that was totally a vacation was Thanksgiving, 1999. My son had moved back to the U.S. to live with his dad, so I took my mother to Kansas City so we could have Thanksgiving with him. This was only technically a vacation in that it did not involve any work. Traveling with my mother is not a vacation. I'd like to build a vacation into a business trip but I've never been able to afford it."

In the sf field, however, business trips are often to interesting places. Ellen and Pat went to Worldcon in Japan a few years ago. I went to Paris four times on someone else's dime (and worked hard, ate plenty, and fell in love with the city).

Award-winning editor, Gardner Dozois, whose *Year's Best Science Fiction* appears every June, points this out in his answer to the question.

He and his wife Susan "went to Australia...and toured there, but a great deal of the initial cost of getting there and back was defrayed by Clarion South, who wanted me to teach, so I guess that was work-related, or at least SF-related."

He has moved to fulltime freelancing in the past few years, and adds, "We may well never be able to afford to have a pure vacation vacation again, although I hope to still be able to do some SF-related things like going to Worldcon, which can be valuable, as a place to scout for work. I picked up a couple of gigs from going to Denver in 2008, for instance."

Like Gardner, I got a lot of work at Denver's Worldcon, and I had a lot of fun too. I don't count such trips as vacations, but I do enjoy them immensely as a way to see friends, stay in touch with the field, and meet people.

But some freelancers quoted above would have counted the Worldcon time as vacation (no writing) and others would not have. It's clear that each freelancer designs her own career, making her own rules, and figuring out what works for her.

Which is what any new freelancer has to do. You can work too much, especially if you're in a high burnout profession, like therapy or broadcast journalism. You can also work too little.

You have to find the balance yourself.

If you can't afford a vacation, take a leaf from Alexandra Honigsberg's book and take a stay-cation. Not all of us live in New York City (sigh), but we all have interesting sights near our homes. I always take my birthday off, and usually, Dean and I go somewhere nearby and see the sights. Last year, we went to Portland, only two hours away, and met up with my sister, showing her Powell's Books and then exploring Old Town, which I had never really visited before.

To answer Jas's question, "How do you justify even one day off?"

You shouldn't have to justify at all. People deserve time off. There's always one more page to write, one more project to finish, one more book to read. There's always a client with an emergency or a news story breaking somewhere. Sometimes you just have to shut off the cell phone, shut down the computer, and go to the beach.

Often, that's more than enough.

Turning Setbacks Into Opportunity

A Freelancer's Survival Guide Short Book

Setbacks happen to everyone. Surviving them is hard. Surviving failure is even harder. But every successful person has had at least three failures before finding that success. So how do you turn failure to success? Read on...

Introduction

We all fail. Sometimes we fail spectacularly. The key isn't preventing failure. The key is picking ourselves up, dusting ourselves off, and moving forward.

Easier said than done, of course. Most of us want to do everything we can to prevent failure.

This short book is three chapters of a huge how-to book called *The Freelancer's Survival Guide*, which was initially published on my blog, kristinekathrynrusch.com. The entire *Guide* is available as both an e- and a paperback book. But this piece will work better if you remember it was initially published as weekly blog posts and written in real time in 2009 and 2010.

Turning Setbacks into Opportunity is part of the *Freelancer's Guide* Short Book series. I carved some of the entries in the *Guide* into short books because not everyone wants *all* of the advice in the larger *Guide*. Sometimes people buy how-to books for one small section. If you're one of those people, then this short book is for you. I hope it answers all of your questions about surviving setbacks, recovering from failure, and using hindsight to solve future problems.

If you want to see how others responded or if you want to see the original posts, go to my blog, kristinekathrynrusch.com, click

Introduction

the tab marked "Business Resources" and select "Freelancer's Survival Guide." That will take you to the table of contents. The posts are clearly marked.

I hope this short book will help you avoid trouble. If you're already in trouble, I hope it'll help you resolve your problems.

—Kristine Kathryn Rusch
Lincoln City, Oregon
July 29, 2010

Setbacks

Let's start by being completely honest: Setbacks hurt. And I don't simply mean that they hurt your business. They hurt personally. They're embarrassing, difficult, infuriating, and terrifying. They make us feel as if this hasn't happened to anyone else before ever, and yet they happen to all of us.

They happen in successful businesses as well as unsuccessful ones. They happen in start-ups and they happen in long-term businesses.

The real key with setbacks isn't preventing them; it's surviving them when they happen. Over the years, I've become a connoisseur of setbacks. I'm not interested in other people's misfortunes (except as a grist for my own fiction), but I am interested in how other people survive those misfortunes.

In other words, I am an inveterate studier of setback recovery. And believe it or not, that's a hard thing to study, since most people hide their misfortunes, and do so very well. They pretend that nothing has gone wrong, and most of us remain fooled, partly because we can't see deeply into other people's lives unless they let us, and partly because we really don't pay attention to anything outside of our circle, unless we're forced to.

I spend a lot of my time imagining what would happen if. In

fact, that's my job. I must imagine what would happen if, because that phrase is at the heart of all fiction. So it's only inevitable that sometimes I turn "what would happen if" from "what would happen if Godzilla suddenly appeared on the Oregon Coast" to "what would happen if I suddenly lost every dime I ever had."

They're not just good exercises for fiction writing; they're good exercises for future planning. Fortunately, my husband, writer Dean Wesley Smith, has the same bent, so he doesn't think I'm ghoulish when I start a "what would happen if" conversation.

In my studies of setbacks and recoveries, I've deduced this: There are four categories and probably a million subcategories of setbacks.

The four major categories are:
1. Financial
2. Mechanical/Technical/Production
3. Physical
4. Emotional

So let's look at them in-depth.

1. Financial Setbacks

The name speaks for itself. For some reason, something happens in the financial side of the business that hurts the business. Did the business undercapitalize? (What the hell does undercapitalize mean, anyway?) Is the business underperforming? Does it pay its bills? (What the hell does paying the bills mean exactly?)

Those are the practical aspects of finances, things that you and your accountant or you and your bookkeeper, or you and the math expert in your family should be able to figure out with a calculator, the invoices, the checkbooks, the bills, and a stack of receipts.

But I'm not referring to that here. In some ways, figuring out the profitability (or lack of profitability) in your business is the easy part.

Turning Setbacks Into Opportunity

The hard part is simpler—and much more terrifying. Something financial that you planned on went horribly awry. Financial setbacks are always a surprise. Maybe not in hindsight, but as they happen, you're usually caught flatfooted. This doesn't mean you can't plan for them, but you'll never know when one is going to strike.

If you've been paying attention to the business news since the fall of 2008, you have heard about setbacks.

Some are extreme. For example, people who invested with Bernie Madoff and the swindlers of his ilk (well, of a lesser ilk, since he seemed to be the master swindler) lost everything. Or the bulk of their savings. Or the money they were going to use to survive their retirement.

In this case, people went from affluent to poverty stricken in the space of an afternoon. Or at least it seemed that way from their perspective. In reality, they went broke the moment they handed Madoff a check.

As an aside: I have little sympathy for people who dealt with Madoff directly. Those people didn't do their due diligence in hiring an outside investor for their funds. Madoff didn't respond well to questions, which is a large red flag. But so many people had invested with a marketing fund or an investment group who then put the money into Madoff as part of a package deal. I feel for those people. I know what it's like to be embezzled from. It's happened to me twice—once a relatively small amount, and once a larger amount. That larger amount had never been in my pocket, however. The embezzler (a book agent) skimmed the money off the top and I didn't even know that money existed. So I didn't miss it when I learned it was gone.

What happened to Madoff's investors is an extreme case. Most people never suffer through that, but they do go through very tough times. The news in the first week of September, 2009, reported that more than one million people lost their jobs since the beginning of 2009. That's more than 125,000 per month—all of whom had just received a financial setback.

That setback is worse for some than others. Some had warning. Others planned ahead and had savings. But for each person who lost a job, the setback is severe. Immediately, the calculations begin: How long until I can't pay my bills? How long before I lose my house?

I've gone through several financial setbacks in my life—from the first (and only) job I've ever been fired from when I was twenty (seems I had an attitude problem [go figure]) to the crash of our publishing company, Pulphouse Publishing, in the early 1990s to some business setbacks that started around 9/11. I honestly don't want to count how many financial setbacks I've survived; just thinking about them makes my stomach twist. I know just how close I was to falling off some kind of horrible precipice, and how each day was a struggle.

But I've never fallen off that precipice. I've always found a way to make money, and I've always had a home. Which is more than my husband can say. He was homeless for a while in his twenties, and he talks about that with understatement. The difficulty of those days, the moment-by-moment panic, must have been agonizing.

Financial setbacks hit businesses as well. From the embezzling employee (like I mentioned above) to the loan that doesn't come through to the big client who goes bankrupt, financial setbacks in a business can be as devastating as the ones in your personal life. In fact, they can lead to financial setbacks in your personal life if you're not careful.

And often, the financial setbacks are related to other setbacks, which I'll talk about later.

How can you protect yourself against financial setbacks?

A. *Plan for them.* I know. I just said they're always a surprise. But I also said that they hit every single business—and they hit every single person at one time or another in life. So have a reserve fund. Have a game plan for tough times. Have contingency plans. Try not to overextend credit to one client. Make sure you have more than one client. Know how much you can afford to lose in one year, so that when a problem does hit, you can assess whether that problem is minor, major, or devastating.

B. *Assess the damage immediately.* When a financial setback occurs, don't think things will get better. Assess where you are now in the new reality, and then plan for things to get worse. Sometimes one financial setback is a precursor to others. (Think of the banks denying all commercial credit in late 2008, and then cutting credit lines. That destroyed a lot of business that use those lines to order stock and stay afloat in the off-season.) Figure out immediately how bad the loss is and how bad it could become.

C. *Cut your losses immediately.* If you lose a major client, don't expect another to take his place. Cut your expenses, cut your salary to the bone, lay off workers if you have to, move to cheaper digs—do whatever you need to in order to compensate for that huge financial loss. The faster you do this, the more likely you are to save your business in the long run.

D. *Search for a way to replace that income.* This, of course, depends on your business. Get another big client, take out a loan from a different organization, sell off some inventory at lower-than-usual prices. Do what you can. If you do C & D in conjunction, you might just turn a financial setback into a blip on the balance sheet.

E. *Be realistic.* If the financial setback damages your business so badly that you are bailing water out of a bottomless boat, then shut the business down. Again, the faster you take action, the better off you'll be. Too many business owners incur tens of thousands of dollars in needless debt by hanging on to a business that will die anyway.

Financial setbacks are often the easiest setbacks to see. Numbers rarely lie. In that way, they're the easiest ones to deal with. You know what's happening—it's all there in black and white. Doing something, however, is harder.

Add to that the feeling of failure that inevitably comes with being unable to meet your obligations or pay your bills, and that's a recipe for disaster.

Talk to the people closest to you. Have a plan. And expect the worst. You'll go through it and come out the other side if you do.

2. Mechanical/Technical/Production Setbacks

These are often product-related setbacks or setbacks that in some way involve the center of your business. For example, grocery stores went through this a few years ago when the government discovered e-coli in spinach. Thousands of dollars worth of produce got tossed, and even more didn't get purchased. Even now, spinach sales are down from their peak before the e-coli debacle.

And imagine what that did to farmers who produced the spinach and the processing plants that packaged the wash-and-eat spinach. Some of those businesses got wiped out, just because some spinach somewhere (and I can't remember where) got contaminated *as it grew*, and so the e-coli was entwined in the actual plant, not on its surface. Who could have planned for that?

A writer I know got a million-dollar book contract, paid out over years and several books. One editor bought those books, then left the company. By the time the writer turned in the first book in the contract (on time, mind you), she had been orphaned three times (meaning three other editors had presided over the project). The new editor who got the book wasn't even familiar with the genre the book was in. My friend rewrote that book to the editor's specifications for another year plus, before the editor decided the book was unacceptable, and asked my friend to repay every dime paid out in the contract thus far.

Think on this: the advance had been paid, the author had done the work—in fact, she'd done three times the normal amount of work—and she still had to repay the money. (She eventually negotiated this down to repayment when she resold the book, which she did—the original version, not the thrice-rewritten thing.)

For two and a half years, this writer made no money and at the end of that period of time, she was told she had to repay money she'd spent three years before. *That's* a setback.

Sometimes mechanical/technical setbacks are the fault of the business owner. My friend could have written a bad book. (In this case, she hadn't, but if she had, then the fault would have been hers.) Some of the e-coli cases in the news lately have been the product of filthy processing plants and uncaring business owners. They're criminally negligent and deserve the punishment they'll be getting.

In some cases, though, setbacks are part of the business. Contractors who remodel houses, for example, never know what they'll find behind ancient walls or underneath a rotted floorboard. And some businesses—like oil drilling—are by nature speculative, with many more failures than successes. Setbacks are planned things in those businesses.

How do you survive a technical/mechanical/production setback?

A. *Have insurance.* Most businesses have insurance for just this sort of thing. If something goes wrong in the manufacture of clothing, for example, then insurance should cover the losses.

A business rider on your insurance policy will help with some of the smaller problems. But not every business can be insured. Writers can't, for example. We have to cope with the occasional failed manuscript, bad agent, or new editor. So the next best thing is—

B. *Make sure you have more than one client or more than one product.* Buggy whip manufacturers never recovered from the switch over to the automobile a century ago, but bicycle repairmen suddenly had a whole new business if they wanted it, because no one knew where to take their car to be repaired, so they went to the bicycle guy, whom they saw as the next best thing to a car repairman. Writers should work for more than one publisher (and in more than one form or genre); stores should carry more than one product.

The more you diversify your business, the better off you are.

C. *Have a contingency plan.* Nothing ever goes entirely as

planned. Assess what'll happen to your business if the main product line has serious problems *before* those serious problems occur. You might be able to turn what could be a setback into a minor problem.

D. *Cut your losses.* Sometimes you try a new product and it doesn't work, for whatever reason. Pull out of that area as soon as possible, and reassess. Make sure you haven't overextended or jumped into an area you didn't fully understand.

E. *Be realistic.* If something went wrong with your machine, or your product, or your timetable, it was probably your fault. Find out where the mistakes were and change that behavior immediately. If the problem wasn't yours, note that. It still had an impact on you, however, and you need to be realistic about whether that impact was minor, bad, or severe.

If you're not realistic, you won't be able to solve the problem. Worse, you won't be able to prevent similar problems in the future.

F. *Take responsibility.* If you're at fault, say so. Offer the client some kind of recompense for the problem. Act swiftly, and the client will usually respond well. (This works except in cases where the problem caused some kind of legal hassle. Then, talk to a lawyer [preferably more than one lawyer] and take his advice.) The faster you own up to a mistake, the more the client is likely to trust you in the future, especially if you do good work from that point forward.

3. Physical Setbacks

Physical setbacks find many forms, but they're always caused by something outside your freelance business acting upon your freelance business.

Some are things the insurance companies call "Acts of God." Fires, earthquakes, floods, tornados, hurricanes are all "Acts of God." You can insure for most of them—you need special insurance for floods, for example—but insurance doesn't stop the setback. It only ameliorates the damage.

Let me explain what I mean. Before I met him, Dean lost his

house to a fire. The fire started in a control panel, and had he been home that day, he could have stopped the damage. But he was out of town, and arrived at the house in time to see the fire department hosing off his collectible books in the front yard.

Dean has always been a big believer in insurance, and he was fully covered for the damages that occurred that day. He got reimbursed for all the lost items, including the collectibles, but some problems that occurred from the fire couldn't be fixed.

In those days, Dean wrote on a typewriter. He lost dozens of manuscripts, many single copies of his publications, and some works in progress. He was too traumatized to go back to the works in progress, even though he could have reconstructed them from scratch, but the lost manuscripts were another matter entirely.

You see, after writing for some time, we writers don't remember our early works very well. Just the other day, I found a story I had forgotten I had written. At Worldcon in 2008, a publisher asked to reprint a story I hadn't though of in nearly 20 years. I reread the story, realized that now I would write it differently, and looked at it as an artifact of another, younger version of Kris. Just as valid, but very, very different.

Most businesses would have some of the same problems. If the collectibles store that we sold a few years ago burned down tomorrow (God forbid), many rare items would be lost. The owner is insured, but the hard-to-find items would be impossible to replace.

Events like this take an emotional toll, just like financial and mechanical/technical/production setbacks do. Even now, reminders of the fire make Dean take a deep breath. We cleared our house of unwanted possessions as we moved our offices, and we found the dishes that Dean had managed to save after the fire. He waved a hand, said, "Get rid of them," and then, not an hour later, changed his mind. He couldn't bear to part with something he had worked so hard to save.

Here's the thing about physical setbacks: There's the event, and then there's the aftermath.

The fire took place in a single day. Dean can still tell you the exact date. But the aftermath took years.

For a larger example, look at Hurricane Katrina. People all over the Gulf Coast lost homes, but they also lost businesses. Areas remained closed for months. Some of those businesses—although insured—never reopened. Some are still being rebuilt.

Imagine losing four years of your life to rebuilding your home and business. It takes a special kind of person to dive in all over again. You have to rebuild your life, of course, but you don't always have to rebuild it in exactly the same way.

Sometimes the physical setbacks don't even have to happen to you or near you. When the planes struck the Twin Towers on 9/11, Dean and I were at home in Oregon. Yet that single event caused a huge ripple through publishing, which is based in New York.

My main publisher at the time was located in an area near Ground Zero, an area that was shut down by the city for more than a month. My secondary publisher lost a number of people in accounting, including the main person who signed the checks. Dean has similar stories.

We did not receive any of the monies owed to us from New York for more than six months after 9/11. We didn't get paid on our contracts—money due to us that September—until March of 2002.

That was a financial setback for us, but it was caused by a physical setback, and my brilliant husband saw it coming. (If you're ever in a disaster, you want Dean at your side. He can see all the implications immediately.)

While I watched television, horrified by the events, and worked the phones and the Internet to see if our friends and colleagues were still alive, Dean piled a bunch of collectible books into our van and drove two hours to Portland. He went to Powell's Bookstore and traded those books for cash. Good thing he did: Powell's shut down its trading arm the next day for some time (a month, I think) and as I said, we didn't get paid for six months.

We didn't need that thousand dollars on 9/11, but we sure

needed it in the weeks that followed. I would never have thought of that, but Dean did, and he acted swiftly.

It's tough to act swiftly in a physical crisis. If the crisis is happening near you or to you, you often can't act swiftly. You're involved in the event, and then you're surviving the aftermath.

Sometimes the very nature of the physical setback—such as Katrina—will cause the aftermath to seem very much like the event. The trauma will continue for some time before recovery can even start.

There's another kind of physical setback, one that can be as bad or worse. You get hurt. If you're the sole proprietor of your business and have no employees, you suddenly have no ability to work either. Even those businesses with employees might not be able to go on for very long without you, because you might be the only one with check-writing ability or the ability to find the jobs or the vision to keep the business on track.

Recently, I was talking with our gardener. He's a strong and able man, who gets more work done in an afternoon than I can imagine. He has at least three employees.

The week before, he was cutting down a holly tree with a chain saw on one of his many job sites. He inspected the tree before cutting it down, looked the area around the tree, and saw nothing amiss. Then he fired up the chain saw and started cutting.

The sound of the saw awoke yellow jackets, which had nested in an underground hollow. He said, "I looked up and saw at least 600 of them heading right toward me."

He jumped, with the chainsaw still going, off the incline he was working on and ran for his truck. Halfway there, he realized the yellow jackets were going for his green shirt, so he pulled the shirt off. Many of the yellow jackets stayed behind, stinging the shirt.

The rest came after him.

He was stung at least 35 times.

To make matters worse, he's allergic to the stings. His assistants drove him from the job site to the nearby hospital, a drive of less than five minutes, and he could barely breathe by the time he got inside the emergency room.

So what did he do?

He took the weekend off. But he was back to work on Monday. He's still puffy, and he says he's downing Benadryl like crazy, but he's working.

The man should be at home. He should be recovering. He should be resting and taking care of himself. But it was summer, his busiest season. He can rest when the rains start in November.

Until then, he's moving through the pain.

His assistant, who helped him get to the hospital and who is at least twenty years younger, is astonished by this. But his assistant doesn't own the business. He doesn't know how important it is to keep working. The assistant—like so many employees—would have the luxury of taking the time off.

Sometimes you can't keep working. Sometimes you have to rest. Sometimes you have to recover. I often say—only half joking—that I could get hit by a bus tomorrow. But I could. And depending on the damage, I might not be back to work for months, if ever.

One more story, and then I'll quit and get to the bullet points. At the age of nine, I fell off my bicycle and landed on my face. I have a lot of physical scarring. Most people don't notice it, but the scarring is severe enough that most plastic surgeons, when they meet me, wave a hand around their face and say, "I can fix that for you if you want."

(I don't want. What I do want is for plastic surgeons to leave me alone.)

I have never fixed the scars, but the teeth needed repair. I had knocked out my front teeth, which were, unfortunately, my permanent teeth. First I had them capped, then they got recapped twice in my twenties. All of these procedures were supposed to be permanent. In my late thirties, the dentists just replaced the front teeth entirely. (That cost money, since I can't get dental insurance because of my pre-existing condition.)

After the first surgery to replace the teeth, I spent a day or so on my back. I'd had dental surgery before, and I planned for those two days off. The third day rolled around, and I stumbled to my desk. Then, I began to cry. I couldn't remember how to write. I thought something in my brain got damaged in the surgery.

Turns out that certain extremely strong pain pills block parts of the brain from communicating with each other. I could want to write, but I couldn't quite figure out how.

I stopped taking the pills. I'd rather hurt than not write. I'm a person with a very high pain tolerance. I can go without pain pills for things that knock most people over.

Most folks wouldn't have been able to forego the medication, and what should have been a few days off might have become weeks.

So how do you handle physical setbacks?

A. *Plan for them*. I know, I know. How do you foresee a disaster like Hurricane Katrina? You don't exactly. (No one could have predicted the bungling that made the results of that storm even worse.)

But you do know the Acts of God that threaten your part of the world. If you live in Southern California, for God's sake, get earthquake insurance. If you live on a historical flood plain, pony up the extra money and buy flood insurance.

Make sure you're insured for fire, and make sure you have a business rider on your homeowners policy.

Insurance isn't enough, however. Most of us, no matter what business we're in, do some work on the computer. Store your backups off site. I keep one current backup of everything in the car and older backups in our storage unit, far from our house.

I'm putting my publications in order as well, and when I have enough, I store the extra copies in the storage unit. That way, if something happens to our house, I can reconstruct most of my published material. I won't get all of it, but I'll get some of it.

Store financial records off-site (in a secure location), and store other important things off-site, as well. For example, I had a computer meltdown earlier this year. The one thing I didn't back up was my e-mail addresses. I'm still reconstructing those.

B. *Assess the damage as quickly as you can.* If you're lucky, you have a mind like Dean's, and can foresee future problems on the day the event occurs. Most of us don't think that way. But as soon as you can, dust yourself off and take stock. Look at the extent of the damage and figure out what it will take to fix everything.

Don't just look at the financial impact. Look at the physical one. Must you rebuild your office? Can you rent an office suite? Are you living out of a hotel? Did the doctor find additional problems in that exploratory surgery?

Get estimates from contractors, talk to your physicians, and then take their timelines and double them. Assume that as the rebuilding happens, something else will go wrong. If you plan for a long setback (like Dean did on 9/11), you and your business will survive the crisis.

You also need to figure out if you'll be able to work during the rebuild. Can you supervise construction and continue your legal practice? Are you clearheaded enough to continue offering therapy to your clients?

These are important questions, not just for your future, but also for the future of your business.

C. *Expect a long aftermath.* Yes, I just dealt with the length of the physical aftermath above, but there's also an emotional aftermath. When my father died, I couldn't work for an entire month. Even though writing was my escape as well as my business, I couldn't get a word on paper. I was grieving and grieving hard. I was trying to make sense of a world without my father in it. It took me some time to reorient myself. I finally got back to work, but I didn't get up to speed for nearly six months.

Dean was still having trouble working when I met him a year after the house fire. The loss of his manuscripts had devastated him. He got work done, but he had trouble believing it would last.

Severe physical events cause emotional trauma. Expect it, be kind to yourself when it happens, and if need be, get some professional help to overcome the most serious effects. You'll be glad you did—and so will the people around you.

D. *Be honest with yourself.* Physical setbacks are often opportunities in disguise. Maybe you felt trapped by your at-home business. Maybe you actually hated going to the store every day. Maybe you aren't really fond of plumbing after all.

If that's the case, use this loss as a chance to start over.

If you still love your work, you might have developed bad habits or overspending. This setback might be the time to rebuild the way you should have built the business in the first place.

Be honest about the business's flaws and try to fix them as you rebuild the business.

E. *Be realistic.* Will the insurance money be enough to rebuild the business? Will your savings cover you while you're recuperating from major surgery? Make sure your assessment of these crucial things is honest and straightforward—and a bit on the pessimistic side.

It's always better to plan for the worst-case scenario. That way, when things aren't as bad as expected, you're actually ahead.

F. *Find a way to replace the lost income.* During the rebuilding period, you might have to get a day job to tide you over. Do so as quickly as you reasonably can so that your basic expenses are covered. This is not a failure. Instead, it's another forward step toward getting yourself and your business back on your feet.

Physical setbacks are a lot more powerful than we give them credit for. They last longer and are often harder to overcome than anyone expects.

4. Emotional Setbacks

In some ways, emotional setbacks are the most difficult setbacks of all. You can blame outside forces for each of the previous three setbacks. For example, you ran into trouble because the economy collapsed. Or because your biggest client didn't pay you. Or because someone sold you tainted spinach to sell to your grocery store customers.

And whose fault was Hurricane Katrina? Even if the government had responded quickly, the hurricane would have still hit the Gulf Coast, ruining countless businesses.

Sometimes, someone else truly is responsible for what happens to you—whether it's an Act of God or someone else's incompetence.

And sometimes, setbacks are your fault.

Face it. We all make mistakes. Sometimes we make doozies. The mistakes might be the result of ignorance or overconfidence, arrogance or inexperience. Whatever the reason, the best thing we can do is own up to our mistakes and not make the same mistake again.

The problem, however, is that you will have an emotional response to any setback that happens to you. Sometimes that response will be relief, which means that you shouldn't rebuild your business in the way that it was before. (Or you shouldn't rebuild it at all.)

But other problems lead to other reactions.

In addition to the physical crisis caused by Hurricane Katrina, that disaster also created emotional setbacks. The survivors grieved. They lost their homes, their businesses, their communities. In many cases, they lost relatives, as well.

Grief is a real, powerful, and sometimes crippling emotion. The grief books (and there are many) recommend going easy on yourself and understanding what you're going through. Survive it, the books say, and eventually you'll feel better.

Which is all well and good when you have a day job that allows you to take personal time or a job that doesn't require your attention every minute of every day. But imagine what it took for these folks to rebuild their businesses and their lives while grieving. They didn't have time to go easy on themselves. They had to work through the grief.

Many people who suffer physical setbacks actually postpone the emotional reaction to it. For some reason (and I'm not a psychologist, so I'm not sure what the reason is), some people can hold back their emotional reaction until a more appropriate time. Soldiers, police officers, and firefighters do this routinely.

Turning Setbacks Into Opportunity

The problem is that when the actual physical crisis ends, the emotional reaction begins. And it's a powerful reaction—all the more powerful because it waited to come out.

That's when you'll hear people apologize for "unnecessary" tears, for "emotional" outbursts, for "inappropriate" anger. The emotional reaction is part of the physical setback and needs to be treated that way. If you skip it—and people do—then the emotion will come out in other ways. Many sufferers of post-traumatic stress disorder never had time to deal with the emotions during the crisis and so have to deal with them when the crisis is over or face a crippling, unpredictable reaction.

If you go through something severe —a fire, a flood, the loss of everything, complete financial collapse—get some counseling, as well. You'll need some kind of support to get through the emotional aftermath, whether that support is through your faith, your friends, or your therapist.

But what of emotional setbacks that have no relationship to the first three setbacks? In some ways, these are the most difficult of all. Because as much as we like to think we're an understanding culture, Americans prefer to ignore deep emotions. We don't want to hear how sad someone is or how angry they became. We might listen sympathetically the first time the story gets told, but if the teller doesn't recover quickly (and we each have a different definition of quickly), then we avoid the topic or worse, avoid the teller altogether.

We have a pick-yourself-up-by-the-bootstraps mentality, and that often means that the people around you expect you to recover right away. The flip side of this are the people who allow one setback to destroy their lives. They find like-minded individuals who never get past whatever it was that destroyed their lives, and they spend the rest of their lives reliving it.

Generally, those in that second group don't have the physical or emotional stamina to own their own business. But most people don't fall into that category. Most people can recover, given time and support. Both of those things are difficult to give, which is why

I recommend that people in crisis get professional help whenever possible.

Generally, the negative emotions cause the most setbacks—although not always. I'll end on a positive emotion that can cause the most trouble of all.

Here's the problem with emotional setbacks, however. Unlike fire that destroys a business or financial meltdown that destroys nest eggs, emotional setbacks aren't always obvious problems. Something emotional that will destroy me won't even bother you and vice versa. Something in our individual makeup causes one type of emotion to hook itself into one person and not bother another person at all.

Take anger. Some people can't abide anger. They fear it. They avoid it in themselves. I've known people who quit jobs because their boss had a quick temper. I used to work for a man who broke phones when he hung up. I worked for a woman who threw dishes while screaming at the top of her lungs. That bothered me, sure, but not enough to quit.

But liars, backstabbers, and manipulators? Whenever they appeared at any job I worked, I quit in an instant. I can't abide people like that, and the smallest incident involving me will make me run from that person forever—paycheck or no paycheck.

Why did I call this difference between people a problem? Simple. Something that might bring you to your knees might strike your best friend as hilarious. It's not that your friend is insensitive. In fact, your friend might be the first on the scene with money and a place to stay if your home and office were leveled in a tornado. But have an emotional tornado, and that friend might not understand what you're going through at all.

When the people around you don't understand, you start questioning your own reaction. Are you overreacting? Are you too sensitive? Are you, in fact, being silly?

Probably not. You're having an emotional setback, and unless you figure out a way around that setback, it might devastate you and your business.

Signs of a severe emotional reaction: inability or lack of desire to go to work, crying jags, extreme (and seemingly unprovoked) anger, and/or something the psychologists call emotional lability—excessive emotional reactions and frequent mood changes.

If these things are happening to you, you'll need to figure out the underlying cause and find a way to release that emotion, or to deal with it, or (worst-case) to block it.

Sometimes, as in the case of grief, you'll just need to endure until the emotional reaction lessens. Time really does heal, although it's hard to realize when you're in the middle of it all.

Often, in the case of emotional setbacks, you're experiencing a problem, but you don't know why. You're less enthusiastic about work. Your habits have changed and you don't know why. You have no joy in something you used to love.

In fact, you may find yourself looking for a way out.

Sometimes, that's a legitimate response to a business you thought you'd like, but you didn't understand or you don't like as much as you thought. Maybe there's more drudgery than you were prepared for or maybe you're not suited to the day-to-day tasks of the business. That's a different issue.

What I'm dealing with here is something more subtle. You've been working at your business for a long while now, and up until lately, you've enjoyed it. Then something changed.

Usually what changed is an event that precipitated an emotional response. So let's look at some of the more common negative emotions and the way they can manifest in your business.

A. *Fear*. Fear is insidious. It paralyzes, quite literally. If you can't get anything done when you used to get a lot done, you might be suffering from excessive fear.

Some of us were raised to be fearful, so this is a natural state. My parents suffered some extreme financial reversals when I was a little girl, and they taught me (through their actions) to quit when the going gets rough. I'll give you one example:

At twelve, I was the best swimmer in my age group at the YMCA, where the local pool was. I won every race among our group. So I represented our group in an actual race against other groups, and as I was swimming, I realized I was half a length behind some other girl. Instead of pushing harder, I climbed out of the pool, claiming I didn't feel well. My parents let me. They took me home, and we never spoke of that race again.

As an adult, I now realize that my coach had the proper response: *Get back in the pool! You're not sick! Keep swimming!* But to me, losing was worse than quitting, so I quit.

I often wonder how different my life would have been if I continued. But my parents, because of their own reversal of fortune (and their reaction to it), told me later I clearly wasn't a swimmer or an athlete. I shouldn't try any longer.

I remained paralyzed with fear over athletics until my late 30s, when I realized that I could finish swim races. Sounds like a minor thing, but it was pretty major for me. Overcoming that fear led to all kinds of other activities, and gave me strength in my writing business.

A lot of us were raised to be perfect, to make no mistakes, so we live in fear of mistakes. We make a single mistake and we freeze, afraid to make another. Instead of charging ahead, we don't do anything.

That's why fear is insidious. You'll lose your opportunity or your advantage or your business because you're taking no action at all. And it's always better to take action, even the wrong action, than it is to remain motionless.

So if you suddenly can't get anything done, ask yourself what you're afraid of. You might be surprised at the result.

B. *Anger.* My favorite emotion. Really. I get a lot done when I'm angry. In fact, anger breaks me out of fear (usually anger at myself). While anger is a driving force for me, it's a paralyzing force for others. Some people—especially women of a certain age—were raised to suppress their anger. Anger was an unacceptable emotion, so they weren't allowed to express it.

If you can't express anger, it comes out sideways—either in snide comments or passive/aggressive behavior. Better to figure out who—or what—you're angry at and confront that person in a non-threatening manner, than to continually punish them with verbal asides or hurtful behavior. Particularly if that person is a client.

Here's the problem with anger, though. It can easily turn into uncontrollable rage. I had to learn how to control my anger and turn it into a positive force. My ex-husband gave me a metal garbage can and told me to kick it every time I got angry over a rejection. Believe it or not, that worked. I loved that can. It dented easily, so I could see the damage. And then I could calm down and write another story or deal in a dignified manner with the person who made me angry. A therapist told me once that she has her clients punch pillows when they're angry. *It gets the violent part of the emotion out*, she said, *and leaves the constructive part.*

It's really not good to own a business with employees and be a shrieker or a person who smashes phones. Extreme anger directed at employees can get you in trouble with the law these days. Better to find a constructive way to deal with it, and then move on.

Sometimes that constructive manner is to get the emotion out, and then fire the employee. Or tell the client you don't want their business any more.

Getting rid of the object of your anger will often make the anger go away.

C. *Betrayal.* This one's hard. Betrayal happens in all kinds of ways. A trusted employee goes to the press with lies. A client badmouths you to other clients. A friend tells your confidences to others who really shouldn't know.

If the person who betrayed you works with you, then often you don't want to go to work even if you own the place. It's easier to avoid that person than it is to confront them about their behavior. And it's easier to avoid work than it is to get rid of the person who hurt you.

Often the best thing to do in the case of betrayal is to take the person who caused the hurt out of a position to hurt you. Don't confide in that friend any more. Fire the employee who went to the press. Refuse new projects with the client who badmouthed you.

And otherwise, don't engage. Let the incident fade into the past. That might seem hard—and it is, initially—but after a while, it gets easier. And then it becomes unimportant.

I wouldn't have believed that last bit twenty years ago. But I've experienced it. And I learned something else.

People forget.

So often, we worry about our reputation. We worry that people will misjudge us or damage our reputation. (Or maybe we damaged it.) Here's the funny thing: Most people never notice. If the harm to the reputation is severe, repair what damage you can and then go on. Over time, it'll be a small part of your résumé if it's there at all.

I haven't edited for 12 years. Recently, a friend of mine interviewed me for a short profile that will appear in a science fiction magazine in a few months. This friend is a student of the field and has known me for at least fifteen years.

He asked me about my writing, about the various genres I publish in, and then asked if I thought we needed to cover anything else. Since the interview was going to go into an sf magazine, I said, "You'll probably want to mention that I won a Hugo for editing *The Magazine of Fantasy & Science Fiction*, and that I used to own (with Dean) Pulphouse Publishing." He laughed, and asked (rhetorically) how he could have forgotten.

He forgot because I haven't done it for so long.

When I was editing, people used to forget that I was also a writer. They see what they want to see—or what you present to them.

Recently, Dean and I asked various writers with long publishing careers how many crashes they had. All of them answered with at least three. Now, these folks were close enough friends that we could even broach the question without apology, and with the exception of one friend, we hadn't seen any of those crashes. And we try to stay current with other people's careers.

Things you think might have an impact on your reputation probably won't harm it at all.

Betrayals that have an impact on reputation probably aren't as severe as you think. Betrayals that are personal will probably make you angry or upset for the rest of your life. But you can't let them make you bitter. Take *constructive* action against the person who hurt you, and then move on.

D. *Failure.* I'm going to do a longer section on failure later on, but failure deserves some mention here. Often we feel like failures when we're not failing at all. What's going on?

Usually, you've failed in a personal dream or goal. Or you've perceived a failure where there is none. Sometimes, it's as simple as attitude.

A friend of mine says that his wife can see a black cloud in every silver lining. I can be that way as well. If twenty-five good things happen today and one bad thing happens, I'll focus on the bad thing. Many people are like that.

When we do workshops, I make the students write down the good things we say about their work as well as the bad things. In fact, I harangue them until they do so.

That's because we often don't hear the compliments. We're looking so hard to improve that we never see what we're doing well.

If you take an attitude of "one mistake is failure" into your business, you won't survive. You really do need to think positively, even if you have to make lists to keep yourself on track. I write down every good thing that happens in my business in my calendar, so when I get into a failure funk, I look back and see the good things. It helps. It really does.

E. *Success.* As with failure, success can sometimes cause an emotional setback.

I know, I know. You're all shaking your heads.

But here's what happens.

You have a goal that you thought was unattainable. That goal is what drives you deep down. You are striving to meet that goal, thinking it'll keep you going for the rest of your career, and then, suddenly, you attain it.

You'll stop working. You won't know why. But you've just lost your driving force.

I've seen this happen countless times. With writers, the goal is usually publishing related. Some writers quit when they sell their first story because they met their goal. Others can't go on after their first (and therefore only) *New York Times* bestseller.

What you have to do in this circumstance is reset your goals. That's not easy, and if you need an unattainable goal, you're going to really have to reach for the stars.

I can't tell you how many people I know who have quit because they attained their driving goal. So if you're having trouble working and you just had a major success, it's time to re-evaluate where you are and what you want from your career.

Emotional setbacks are as real as any other kind of setback. They're sometimes harder to identify, and often harder to overcome. But you can do it.

My philosophy about any kind of setback is simple: It doesn't matter how many times you fall down. Nor does it matter how long you remain sprawled on the floor. The only thing that matters is how many times you get back up.

The key to setbacks is twofold: expect that you'll have some over the years, and figure out how to survive them.

And if you really want something, you can survive anything.

Failure

Since I've been dealing with setbacks, I suppose I should go all the way, and talk about failure. Failure isn't something I'm fond of, but not for the reason that you think.

I happen to believe in failure. I think that we learn by failing. Watch any child learn how to walk and you'll realize that it's all about failure. No child gets up and walks the first time he is set on his feet. Children pull themselves to their feet, then fall on their butts. Then they pull themselves up, take a tentative step, and fall.

We as adults know that it's only a matter of time before the child starts scurrying across the living room toward the collectible books (better move them to a higher shelf *now*), but the child doesn't know that. Still, he tries, and tries, and tries.

I've watched my siblings and my friends raise their children. I've seen a lot of kids in this stage, and I've noticed something. The parents who comfort the child when he falls, *especially if he's not crying,* actually impede his development.

One afternoon in the early 1980s, I was at my grandmother's house with my mother and a cousin who had a year-old boy. (I think it was my cousin; it might have been a neighbor. I'm hazy about whose child I actually was watching that day.) The boy was pulling himself up and then falling, and he was making his way around the dining room, standing, taking a step, falling; standing, taking a step, falling.

My grandmother had a non-intervention policy with her children and her children's children. She gave her opinion when asked, but didn't volunteer much. Or maybe she did, but certainly not in front of others. When I got married the first time, she supported me. When I got my divorce, she was there for me (even though she was getting frail). When I met Dean, she pulled me aside and said, "This is a good one. You keep him."

Not only was that the best advice she ever gave me on my personal life, it was one of the only direct pieces of advice she ever gave.

So what I'm about to tell you remains clear in my memory because of my mother and my grandmother, not because of that little boy trying to walk.

We four women were talking and keeping an eye on the boy, when suddenly he pulled one of the chairs over. It knocked him down, but didn't hit him. He sat in the middle of the floor, unhurt but startled, with that lovely expression startled toddlers get: *Do I cry? Should I cry? Did this really bother me?*

He had already decided it didn't bother him and had reached for the next chair to help him stand up as my mother ran to his side, checking in a great panic to see if he was all right. The boy's mother, seeing my mother react, hurried to the boy, too.

The boy started to cry. He didn't just cry. He wailed and sobbed and it took them nearly fifteen minutes to calm him down.

When the drama was over, my grandmother looked at my mother. "Marian," my grandmother said, "if you had left that boy alone, he wouldn't have even noticed that he had fallen."

"But he might have been hurt," my mother said.

"He wouldn't have noticed that either," my grandmother said, and then changed the subject.

I was startled at two things. First, that my grandmother had spoken up. As I said, she had a non-intervention policy. But second, her insight from (by that point) almost seventy years of child rearing and child watching struck me as true.

Children, raised in loving homes with parents less nervous than my own, fail easily and rarely notice. They take spills, and then they get up. They drop a ball, miss a catch, or trip over a crack in the sidewalk, and they laugh as they try again.

We let toddlers do this. In fact, we let children do this up to the age of three or so. We know that the try-and-fail method works, and that the child will eventually speak and walk. We gently guide our children by telling them no when they get near a hot stove, by steering them away from an aunt's favorite glass vase, by holding their hand as they cross the street.

But we accept the try-and-fail model.

And then the child goes to school.

I don't know when this happened, but it happened after I graduated from college but before my friends started sending their children to school in the 1990s. Suddenly, everyone got gold stars and encouragement. Kids didn't fail classes and rarely got Ds.

College professors I know started complaining about this, because these kids often got their first D in college. Or, God forbid, their first F. And you'd think the world had ended.

My sister, a professor, visited me in Oregon shortly after her semester ended. A few nights into the trip, she was still dealing with a student who was protesting his less-than-stellar grade, a grade she said he deserved. (And I believe her. She's the tough but tender teacher who taught me how to read and gave me some of my most favorite novels.)

Why am I going on about this? Because failure is something we need to practice. Handled well, failure leads to success. In fact, I know of no long-term successful businessperson who lacks a failure in her background.

Don't believe me? Think about this: Henry Ford went bankrupt five times before starting Ford Motor Company. Walt Disney's first cartoon studio went bankrupt.

Read the biographies of successful people. Some of these biographies will focus on the failures, and show them for the learning experiences that they were. The show *Biography* on A&E skips over the failures by mentioning them and then saying, "Five years later…" or placing a commercial break between the failure and the next success. Your job, as someone who studies how successful people do things, is to find out what happened in those intervening five years and figure out how that person who is famous enough for A&E to waste an hour of air time on them turned that failure into a success.

That's why I was initially reluctant to title this post "failure." I don't believe in failure. Not really. I know it happens. I know that it's part of life. But I also know that failures are opportunities.

Opportunities to start over. Opportunities to make changes. Opportunities to learn.

And that's the key. Like the toddler who has fallen on his butt, you could sit there and cry and wait for someone to pick you up. Or you can reach for the next chair, haul yourself to your feet, and stagger forward.

A few weeks ago, a friend asked me if I made a mistake when I married the first time. I startled him by saying I didn't make a mistake at all.

Now, knowing that my first marriage ended in divorce, you'd think that I would acknowledge the failure and say that I shouldn't have married my first husband at all.

But I would have lost so much. I would have lost several good years of a friendship I valued. I would have lost lots of learning experiences, and I would never have walked the road that led me to this moment, to this part of my life.

Joyce Carol Oates writes in her essay "Nighthawk" about her failure to qualify as a PhD candidate at the University of Wisconsin. The essay is a rumination on failure and its importance, but also on the opportunities that it brings.

Most things that people identify as failures aren't failures at all. They're setbacks, which I dealt with in the previous essay. Setbacks turn into failures when you let them defeat you. When they crush you and keep you from achieving your dreams.

That said, I have failed many times in my life. I've been failing for the past month. I've been trying to write a novella that I have had to restart four times. That's right. I've failed at writing this damn thing four separate times.

But is that going to stop me? No. I'll keep trying until I get it right.

That's a small failure. But I've had larger ones. I've gotten divorced, and in the process hurt the man I loved enough to marry. I've been fired. I've had two businesses fail. I've had two separate people embezzle from me. I've had two people who I thought were close friends actively try to destroy my business.

I count all of those things as failures. I've responded well to some of them and terribly to others. I've survived them all. I'm sure I'll survive many more.

Because that's the key to failure. Unless the mistake(s) you made actually kill you, you will survive. Whether or not you live with those mistakes is your choice. Whether or not you use them to better your life is also your choice.

In her essay, "Nighthawk," Joyce Carol Oates says that had she gotten that PhD, she wouldn't have written the work that has made her one of our most distinguished artists. If I hadn't gotten the divorce, I wouldn't have started Pulphouse Publishing, edited *The Magazine of Fantasy & Science Fiction* or written one-tenth of the stories I've written. Because Dean has been beside me in all of those ventures, and sometimes he's the one who has dragged my very best work out of my closed fists and given me the courage to mail it.

Did that toddler fail when he pulled the chair down all those years ago? No. He learned that chairs aren't as stable as he thought and that they could be dangerous. (He also learned that if he gives women of a certain age a watery startled look, he'll get hugged [whether he wants the hug or not]).

As tough as it is, we all have to learn how to accept failure in our lives. For some of us, we have to bring it back into our lives.

How do you deal with failure? Honestly, that was what the

essay on setbacks is all about. At the time it occurs, a setback is a potential failure. It becomes a failure if you never move forward.

As I prepared to write this section of the guide, I looked up the word "failure" in the indices of my business books. Most avoid the topic altogether, which is a shame. Only one deals with it at all.

That single book is, believe it or not, *The Complete Idiot's Guide to Getting Rich* by Larry Watchka, published in 1996. Watchka has one paragraph on failure.

He writes, "Fear of failure will kill your business. You should always ask yourself, 'What is the worst thing that can happen?' Next, you should ask yourself, 'Can I handle the worst thing?' If the answer is yes, then don't worry about it any more. Make plans to handle the worst thing, and then eliminate the fear."

It sounds so easy, but it's hard. Most of us had the fear of failure pounded into us. We're supposed to "get it right the first time." We should "avoid mistakes at all costs." We're supposed to be perfect.

As if perfection is even possible. It's not. We all know it—at least when we're watching toddlers. We know that they'll try and fail. Just like we know that they'll eventually succeed. Because unless they have serious health problems, all toddlers learn how to walk eventually. You just have to give them the time and the breathing space to do so.

You have to do that for yourself, as well. You have to expect the mistakes and expect the failures. Plan for them.

Then change your attitude. You could focus on the failures. I didn't have to marry again. I could call myself a loser because my first marriage failed. Or leave publishing because my first publishing company failed. Or quit writing because my first novel got rejected (many, many times).

Instead, I deal with the failure, call it a setback, and move on. That's why I hate the word failure. It has such finality to it. A failure is only a failure if you let it become one. Otherwise, it is an opportunity.

Or, as Winston Churchill once said (Churchill, who lost most of his fortune in the Crash of 1929 and had to go back to work),

"Success is the ability to go from failure to failure without losing your enthusiasm."

Yep. And if you do lose your enthusiasm, you struggle to regain it. I've had that happen, too.

That's why I insist you should only freelance at something you love. Because there will be times when the only thing that gets you through the day is the fact that you love the work. Not that you love the fame or the money or your co-workers. But that you love the work itself.

This chapter is deliberately short because I don't like to dwell on failure. I like to figure out what went wrong, and then move right past the difficulty, heading to the good stuff. I reach up to grab the next chair so that I can toddle on my merry way.

So toddle on, my friends. If you keep that in mind, you will become a success.

The Benefits of Hindsight

I don't know if we get wiser as we get older, but we certainly gain a lot more experience. The experience comes in handy, if we choose to use it. And sometimes that experience is just there, a part of our personal history and nothing more.

I had a discussion with someone recently about hindsight. We both discussed our fathers, both of whom discouraged us from our first marriages. The person I was talking to is going through a divorce right now. I went through mine 24 years ago.

We both agreed, in the course of our conversation, that our fathers had been right. We also agreed that if we had looked at those relationships now—from the outside (with someone not us) and with the benefit of another couple decades of living—we would see the upcoming problems, as well.

Relationships follow patterns, and people often get attracted, particularly early on, to someone who might give us an opportunity to heal problems that currently exist in our own lives. Watching other people's relationships has given me insights into my own. But that all comes from experience (and an annoying tendency toward nosiness).

The conversation with my friend wasn't a bitter one, though. In fact, we both laughed about our poor fathers' inability to stop us, and we both expressed some empathy for our fathers in that situation. Because as clearly as our fathers could see the situation, their experience didn't extend to preventing it.

Then, of course, both of us contemplated what might have happened had we listened to our fathers. If I hadn't married the first time, I would probably never have met my current husband. If I hadn't met Dean, I certainly wouldn't be typing this now.

As I've said before, I don't regret that first marriage, despite the pain and anguish it caused me and my ex. Not only do I (we, I hope) have some good memories, but that relationship was a critical one in forming both of us. Fascinatingly to me is this: Had my ex and I stayed together, his children would never have been born. Had we done things "right," he would have lost the family he has now, and probably not had a different one in its place. I never wanted children, which we discussed at the beginning. My ex, at nineteen, figured (without telling me) I'd change my mind.

I never did.

Most of us use hindsight the way I did here, to explore the various possibilities of our lives, the paths not taken. I actually looked at that very topic in a story I just published in *Analog*, called "Red Letter Day." The idea being if you could write a letter to your younger self, helping that person either change something in their life or not, what would you write? Would you write at all? (Still haven't entirely answered that one for me.)

But we can use hindsight for more than what-if exploration. We can use hindsight as we build our businesses. In fact, I believe hindsight is an essential tool of business-building.

What changes a failure to a setback? Attitude. I know a number of people, several of them men, who have not remarried after their divorces. Most of those men never even dated again. They were so rocked by the failure of their marriages that they simply could not conceive of another relationship at all. They weren't willing to try again.

Sometimes, this attitude is healthy. It comes from suffering physical pain. It's hardwired in. When we get hurt badly, we don't want to repeat the behavior that caused us that pain. This makes sense when it comes to touching a hot stovetop with your bare hand—you're not going to do that again if you can at all help it—but makes a lot less sense when applied to everything in life.

If we avoided everything that hurt us, emotionally and physically, over the years, we'd eventually stop doing anything. I've turned my ankle crossing a room without tripping on anything; does that mean I shouldn't walk again?

Back in the failure chapter, I used the analogy of the child learning to walk. Toddlers don't give up. They want to move on their own too much to stop, even though they fall constantly and often hurt themselves.

But that's a simple analogy. I don't think (don't remember, honestly, and don't really know) whether toddlers analyze what made them fall. I suspect toddlers just get right back up and try again without any real thought except some version of *I'm going to conquer this thing; everyone else I know has.*

That bullheadedness serves us well in many areas of life. Sometimes, you need to get right back on the horse, the bike, whatever cliché you prefer.

And sometimes, you need to analyze what went wrong. You need to use hindsight.

Because I have a driving desire not to ever make the same mistake twice, I get really angry at myself when I do make a single mistake over and over again. I don't quit whatever it is I'm doing—I'm closer to that bullheaded toddler than I let on in public—but I do rethink it, and sometimes I take a vacation from it.

Case in point: Business. Business, unlike writing, is something I learned as an adult. I'm a very organic writer. I read, gather information, and eventually apply it. I can teach what I've learned—somewhat. But as I recently explained to a group of professional writers who had all come to study with me, if you delve too deeply into my ability to express my knowledge about writing, you'll learn that my ability to describe what I know is pretty shallow. At some point, I just shake my head and say, "Look, just do it. If you can't do it, then we'll see what else we can figure out." Not because I'm frustrated with the student, but because my own learning process in that area is so subconscious that I can't even articulate how I know what I know. And sometimes expressing what I know is equally hard.

On the other hand, I learned business in the school of hard knocks. And when I say hard knocks, I mean the kind that make little cartoon birdies and stars revolve around your head for years. I can point out each wound and scar, each dent to my thick skull, and every single slight that every happened, my fault or not.

Why am I not bitter? Sometimes I am. I occasionally indulge in the pity party or the nasty analysis of someone who has hurt me years ago. But mostly, I learned relatively young that looking backwards and wallowing in regret does me no good whatsoever.

Life moves forward whether we want it to or not. Our choice is whether to move with it or to give situations the permission to batter us around.

Hindsight is the tool that allows us to move forward. It is also the tool that allows us to go near a stove again. We assess what went wrong, and then we see if it's even possible to move forward again without repeating the same mistake.

Once you put your hand on a hot stovetop, you realize that you have to approach that stove with caution. A toddler might stay away from the stove entirely, since a toddler can't see the top, and judges the entire thing harmful and can't yet understand a stove's benefits.

But an adult realizes that there are many ways to approach that stovetop, most of which will not hurt, if you're careful. One thing most of us do, however, is keep our bare hands away from any part of the stove that's on. Most of us never put our hands on that top without looking at it first.

Simple caution, based on experience. It allows us to have a useful, if dangerous, item in our home.

But let's move hindsight away from the realm of the physical into the realm of the mental. Pain can be emotional. The emotion comes from severe stress and trauma.

I've owned many businesses, and I've failed at a lot of them. I've

Turning Setbacks Into Opportunity

approached each one with the idea that I won't make those same mistakes again. Often, I decided not to go into the same kind of business again.

When Dean decided to open a collectibles store as a hobby, I wanted nothing to do with it. I had worked retail from the age of twenty forward, and my ex and I owned a frame shop and art gallery that was a retail shop.

I hated most of the aspects of owning a store. I hated the hours. I hated the stuff. I hated the cash outlay required to get inventory, to rent (or buy) a building, and most of all, I hated waiting for customers to come in.

But Dean had owned several shops, and had loved them. I was not about to stop him from doing something he loved. So I helped him plan, using the mistakes my ex and I had made in the past, combining those mistakes with the ones Dean made in his early stores.

That planning, and all of that hindsight, allowed us to build a successful business. I didn't ever stand behind the cash register, but I was part owner. Dean and I made the major decisions together.

Our experience paid off. Dean's expertise in collectibles made the store a destination stop within its first year. The inventory came from Dean's collections, and his judicious purchases of other people's collections.

Because Dean knows himself quite well, he also realized that the joy in any project for him is building that project. He literally built this business from scratch, making a deal with an owner of a strip mall that we would pay to fix up a dilapidated space inside that mall in exchange for three years of rent.

The nice thing about that rent deal and the previously owned inventory is that together, they gave us the opportunity to walk away from the business if it didn't work. We had three years of free rent, so we had three years to see if the business could sustain itself. We had more than a year's worth of inventory, so we had relatively few start-up costs.

The business became so successful so quickly (which we did not expect) that Dean realized he was going to have to put more time into it than he had planned. That realization too came from experience. He had done this before, and he knew how to grow a business. He did not want to become a collectibles mogul. This was supposed to be his hobby, not his life.

Once he made that realization, he sold the business—for a profit—six months after Oregon, already ahead of the curve, had sunk into this deep recession. The new owner, who had worked at the business from the start, maintained it, and it continues to grow even now, doing extremely well in this tough economic climate.

Every single plan we made about that new business came from hindsight. We knew, first of all, that Dean needs to build things. He always has something going on besides his writing. Before he wrote, he had two or three new things happening, as well. He must create on a variety of levels, and it's impossible to hold him back—although he's great at analysis and able to figure quickly if a new project is the right project for him.

That ability to figure out if a new project is right also comes from experience. In our lifetime together, he's started projects only to abandon them within the week as it became clear that he wasn't suited for them. Time has taught us to evaluate first, sink money in later.

Experience taught us to do the financial plan up front. We'd both started businesses by the seat of our pants, with just a vague idea that it would work out. Once or twice it did, but mostly it failed.

We also learned that we needed to spend as little on start-up as possible because we were taking no outside investors. We needed to be able to walk away from this business. Because of our years of experience we knew that the economy was headed downward (long before the "smart guys" in Washington had it figured out), and we had to make the business as recession-proof as possible. We'd both started businesses in a recession, and we lost Pulphouse Publishing in part because of our response to the recession of 1992. So we knew how dangerous the overall economic climate could be to a business.

We planned for that.

We also knew the price we needed if we decided to sell the business, and we knew it up front. Mostly, we expected to shut it down if it didn't work. The fact that we found a buyer with little effort had more to do with Dean's planning abilities than with mine, but he doesn't like building things only to take them apart. So he worked hard to keep potential buyers interested, even while he started the business up.

All of this planning was extremely different from the planning we had done in our early businesses. Those, as I said, were done without enough planning at all. In fact, I didn't understand why places like the Small Business Administration wanted a business plan. How could we know how the business would operate when we hadn't operated a business?

I recently watched a business go through the same by-the-seat-of-their-pants start-up, and I haven't even talked to or met the owners. I recognize the signs from experience alone.

Down the hill from our house, a lovely Italian restaurant went out of business but not because of financial mismanagement. The place was wildly successful. Instead, it closed because of what I think of as a weird Oregon Coast phenomenon. The owners got sick of tourists.

We went to this restaurant a lot, and in hindsight, the signs of the closure were obvious. It started when the owner decided that locals could make reservations, but tourists could not. Then it migrated to little signs on the table, telling people to control their children and not to use their cell phones. Then the hours got strange—staying open on Monday and Tuesday (traditionally days on the Oregon Coast when business are closed because there are no tourists) and closing on Sunday. In their last year, the owners closed for the summer (the high season) and reopened in the winter (when the town is empty). The reopening didn't last. In fact, the restaurant closed for good during, of all things, spring break.

The owners loved to cook. They loved to cook for people they liked. They hated dealing with rudeness, demands, and all the other things that come with owning a restaurant.

They had owned their building, and it sat empty for two years, waiting for a buyer or for someone to rent it.

This spring, someone rented it.

Because the restaurant is so close to us, we watched the newcomers build it. A small sign went up immediately, announcing the future home of the new restaurant. The front door sat open during the business day, as the new owner painted and did a slight remodel. The official sign went up in late May and with it, an announcement on the changeable sign below, that the restaurant would open on June 25.

Well, I could see the interior of that place, and it was clear to me that they would have to push to hit their June 25 deadline. On June 20, the furniture got delivered. On June 24, the sign changed to a July 2 opening. Fourth of July is the biggest weekend in our little tourist town, so it became clear that these new restaurateurs wanted to take advantage of that.

But both Dean and I have worked in restaurant start-ups, and we know that a menu, a good chef, and a well-designed interior do not a restaurant make. Every single successful restaurant that we've worked at—and that Dean has managed—has given itself a month to work out the kinks. Mostly, the restaurant holds practice nights with the newly hired wait staff, without opening the restaurant at all. When I was a teenager in Superior, Wisconsin, one restaurant invited the relatives of every single person on the staff to come into the restaurant and *eat free* for Thursday, Friday, and Saturday night. That restaurant did so for two weeks.

By the time it opened, the staff knew the menu, knew the quirks of the kitchen, had made (and corrected) dozens of errors, learned where everything is kept, and learned how to pace themselves through a restaurant slammed with customers.

(Our local six-plex movie theater did the same thing, by the way, just to get the bugs out of their system.)

Dean worked varieties of the same practice session. Every restaurant that does this opens to acclaim, if not for the food, at least for the service.

On July 1, the restaurant below announced a July 5 opening date.

On July 4, the opening date was gone.

On July 17, the place held a stealth opening. They'd lost an entire month of revenue from their business plan (if indeed they had one), and they have so far gotten no word of mouth throughout the community. The stealth opening allowed them to practice a little, but they probably lost customers who expected a more polished staff/restaurant.

I hope they'll survive, but the cold opening probably made things harder than they needed to be. And the cold opening is a clear sign of inexperience.

So, how do you make hindsight work for you?

1. Do a fearless inventory of what went wrong in your previous business(es)

Make a list and *be honest*. If you're not honest, there's no point. If you did something wrong, or several somethings wrong, admit them. You need to understand where *all* of the mistakes are, not just some of them.

2. Evaluate whether the mistakes came from…

a) the economy; b) your response to the economy; c) your inexperience; or d) your personality. If the mistakes came from the economy, then you'd better make sure you know how to weather the same economic climate. If they came from your response to the economy, then you'd better learn how to be more flexible in response to a crisis.

If the mistakes came from your inexperience, don't get overconfident. Just because you have experience now doesn't mean you're all wise. Plan to make more errors.

If the mistakes came from your personality, you'd better find a way to negate that part of you that has the tendency to do things wrong *for the type of business you're opening*. I'm great at publishing and editing, but I'll never edit again. I'm good at it, but not suited to it. No amount of "change" will make me and editing suit. I might be able to do a small project or two, but I won't make a career out of it—not without a personality transplant. Been there, done that, spent enough to buy a factory's worth of T-shirts.

If the mistakes came from your personality, you might need to hire someone to take that part of your personality out of play. I could own a publishing company (in partnership with Dean) again, if I don't edit. But I would have to remain hands-off with the new editor. I would have to trust that person—which is a tall order. As I said, I'm very good at editing, and I'd see mistakes right off. I'd probably drive that person out of the business if I weren't careful.

Hiring a person to do the part of the job you're not suited for has all the pitfalls of hiring an employee for other aspects of your life. Employees often create problems instead of solving them.

If your previous business failed due to your personality, then you might want to reconsider stepping back into that same kind of business at all. Sometimes it's better to say that you don't suit than it is to keep pounding your head against the same brick wall.

3. Use Other People's Hindsight

Ask them about the mistakes they made in the same type of business. Do this even if you've owned a business before. You'll learn something, guaranteed.

However, make sure you listen to their advice. At least three start-up publishers interviewed me and Dean about what went wrong at Pulphouse Publishing. We were very honest with them, told them about various warning signs, and told them to call us if things got dicey.

All three of those start-ups failed, one spectacularly. All three of them followed the exact same path that Pulphouse followed, and all three responded to the problems the same way we did—which is to say, the wrong way.

They were forewarned. Of course, they took no notes during our meeting, never contacted us when things got dicey, and only one remembered our advice at all. He later admitted to us that he was in the hospital (the failure caused a physical collapse that put him in the hospital for weeks) and he kept hearing our voices, telling him what exactly would go wrong if he didn't take our advice. He says we haunted him, and he apologized for not listening.

He didn't owe us an apology. He owed himself one.

4. Let Hindsight Help You in All Aspects of Your Business

Because I know how a failing business behaves, I often will not work with a business that is exhibiting the symptoms of a business on the edge. Because we had a publishing house collapse, I particularly know the signs of that, so I won't approach a company that even whispers of trouble. The trouble is often obvious to those of us who have been through something similar years in advance.

In fact, when Dean and I talked with one of those start-ups all those years ago, the owner told us in the middle of the meal he was buying us that he "would never ever make such dumb mistakes." We immediately decided never to work with him—not because he insulted us, but because his ego was so large that he believed he was immune to our stupidity.

He compounded our stupidity, and his failure was so spectacular that people within publishing still discuss it as an example of what not to do when running a business.

5. Remember the Most Important Lesson of Hindsight: You Are Fallible

Sorry, kiddo. You'll make mistakes just like the rest of us. In fact, you'll make mistakes every single time you start a new business. You'll make mistakes after owning that business for ten years, fifteen, twenty. Face it: You'll make mistakes.

This is where I get my mantra. The key is to avoid making the same mistake *twice*. You'll always make new mistakes. Be creative about them. Make new mistakes in the pursuit of the perfect, mistake-free business. Then learn from those new mistakes.

That's what hindsight is for. Toss out the regrets and the "I wish I hads." Stop fantasizing about going back in time and fixing things.

Move forward with the right attitude—after you've fearlessly looked backwards, of course—and you'll have success.

Goals & Dreams

A Freelancer's Survival Guide Short Book Second Edition

We all dream, but only a handful of us know how to make our dreams come true. This short book will help you turn your wishes into reality.

Introduction

Everyone has dreams. Most of us have goals. However, many of us don't realize when our goals cross into our dreams or even get in the way of them. And most of us don't know how to make our dreams a reality.

These posts from my *Freelancer's Survival Guide* discuss how to turn your dreams into achievable goals. The posts also examine whether or not to postpone your dreams as well as figuring out when you're giving up on yourself.

Since April of 2009, I have written *The Freelancer's Survival Guide* on my blog, kristinekathrynrusch.com. Most of the advice in the *Guide* is practical—how to set up a business plan, for instance. *The Freelancer's Survival Guide* is also available in book form.

However, I've also divided the *Guide* into short books for people who don't need or want more than one section. Again, most of those short books involve business things, like handling finances or how to negotiate a contract. But this book is a little different. It's about the emotions of freelancing, about dreams and wishes and aspirations. In other words, this short book is the important one.

These posts were written at separate times throughout the course of a year. I've tried to keep the flavor of the real-time posting, while making sure the book itself has a flow. If you want to see the

Introduction

original blog posts, you can find them—and reader comments—on the blog itself.

The point of this short book, however, is to help you achieve your dreams. I hope it does that and so much more.

Enjoy.

—Kristine Kathryn Rusch
Lincoln City, Oregon
August 29, 2010

I updated the "Giving Up On Yourself" section in 2011 on my website. Things are changing dramatically. It took longer than I expected to update this book, but now I have, and I hope that makes it even more useful for you.

—<i>Kristine Kathryn Rusch</i>
April 19, 2012

The Difference Between Goals and Dreams

We use the words "goals" and "dreams" interchangeably. We achieve our goals, pursue our dreams. We pursue our goals, achieve our dreams. But goals and dreams are very different. A shorthand way of thinking about this comes from football.

That weird little H-shaped thingie sticking out of the end zone? It's called a *goal*post, not a *dream*post. I think football would be an entirely different game if it had a *dream*post. Hockey would be different too, if the players tried to get the puck past the dreamer.

In fact, the difference between a goalie and a dreamer are as illustrative as the difference between goalpost and dreampost. As I go on here, playing with words, you're starting to get an inkling of what I'm talking about.

Goals, simply put, are something you achieve. My *Encarta World English Dictionary* gives me five definitions of "goal." Four are connected to sports, including number five, which is "the end of a race." Number four is the only non-sports related definition of the word: "something that somebody wants to achieve."

Achieve. We achieve our goals. Goals are an end product. The other definitions include phrases like "a successful attempt at..." or "the score gained..."

There are no words like "successful" or "gained" in the definition of dream. Nor does the definition of dream include the word "achieve."

The same dictionary gives the noun "dream" six definitions, and most of them involve sleep or inattention or thoughts. First, of course, the dictionary discusses those visions our mind serves up when we're sleeping. It also discusses the daydream.

The two definitions that concern us are the third and the fourth. I'm going to start with the fourth: "An idea or hope that is impractical or unlikely to ever be realized." If that were the definition of goal, then every single sports team in the world would be in trouble. (Of course, I've known a few football teams bad enough to make a win an impractical hope.)

The third definition is a little more upbeat: "Something that somebody hopes, longs, or is ambitious for, usually something difficult to attain or far removed from the present circumstances."

Ah, now we're getting somewhere. And since I try to be very practical in the *Guide*, and you all seem to recognize that, you probably think I'm going to tell you to abandon your dreams and set goals.

Nope.

Both dreams and goals are necessary for success. You just have to understand the difference between them.

Deep down understand it.

I don't think a freelancer can survive long without a dream. I think the more impossible the dream the better. If you don't set that impossible dream high enough, you'll achieve your dream and stop striving.

When students apply for the Master Class that my husband, Dean Wesley Smith, and I teach (along with four other established professional writers), we ask those students what their goals are and what their secret, most impossible dream is. The only students we take for the Master Class are those with either a professional career that has stalled (for some reason) or those with a strong work ethic who are having trouble breaking into publishing (and have excellent, professional-level skills).

Goals & Dreams

We look at the goals and the secret dream more than any other part of the application. Because if the goals and the secret dream are nonexistent, we have learned that the writers often don't have the capability to survive the Master Class, let alone the business of writing itself.

What does an impossible dream add to a career? Purpose. Plain and simple. That dream is like the shining city on a hill, the one you can see in the distance and might never reach. But until your dying day, you'll head for that hill.

The other thing that the impossible dream adds is a sense of hope. As long as you have something grand to strive for, you also have something grand to hope for. Hope gets us through the dark times better than anything else.

When hope disappears, so, too, does drive.

Which is why it's so hard to succeed on a long-term level if you have easily achieved dreams. If you lack that one huge impossible dream. Because you might reach that city on the hill within the first few years of your professional career. And then, what will you do? What will you hope for? What will you daydream about?

I think the daydream part is also essential. You need something to entertain your imagination while you're working day to day. If you're an actor, you might spend time every day studying fancy gowns for your trip down the red carpet for your tenth Oscar nomination. Not your first, not your fifth, your tenth. Your impossible dream might be to have more Oscar nominations than Meryl Streep.

But if your impossible dream as an actor is to have a small part in a film—well, you might achieve that dream the day you sign up as an extra in a large crowd scene. That's a dream you can attain in my tiny town on the Oregon Coast. Dozens of movies have been filmed here since I've lived here, and lots of locals have had their mugs on the screen, if only for a few seconds. A few of the locals actually had small speaking parts. Heck, my husband's best friend— an attorney—had a speaking role in a commercial filmed in Idaho. Because of that thirty seconds on the nation's television screens, our attorney friend is one of Idaho's members in the Screen Actors Guild.

Had his lifelong dream been to become an actor—someone who qualified for the Screen Actors Guild—then he did so in a single outing with a single commercial. But if his lifelong dream had been to become a famous star of stage and screen, someone who had not just an Oscar, but also an Emmy and a Tony, someone who had a lead role on Broadway, as well as starring roles in hit movies or hit TV shows—well then, he has a long, long way to go.

See the difference? Even those things I listed above might not be enough for that impossible dream. An actor might want to be considered the greatest actor of his generation. A writer might want to have the bestselling book of all time. A storeowner might want to create the largest store franchise in the world.

Because these are dreams, not goals, it's okay to noodle on them, to see them as a shining light in the distance, as something to work toward, but not something to count on.

Goals, on the other hand, are stepping stones. Goals must be achievable. Goals should build on each other.

Go back to the football analogy. A football game in which a score is just a dream would be the dullest thing on the planet. In fact, football players wouldn't even have to face off. They could sit on the field, if they wanted, and imagine the score. Of course, no one would come to the game—because there wouldn't be a game. Just a dream of a game.

But football is a game of inches. It is built on phrases like "first and goal." The game itself sets up tiny goals that lead to a touchdown. And if the team fails in one tiny goal, then the ball goes to the other team, which then tries to achieve a series of small goals to get to the larger one.

The dream for football players isn't to win one game. A lot of players achieve that as early as the age of eight or ten, in a Pee-Wee Football League. Or they have the game-winning run (or the game-winning pass) as early as the first game of their high school career.

The dream for football players is to play in the Super Bowl. Or

Goals & Dreams

to win the Super Bowl. Or to be the Super Bowl's Most Valuable Player—not once, but several times throughout their career.

That's a dream that can't be achieved without a lot of goals—small and large. From getting on the varsity team in high school, to playing well enough to stay, to winning game after game, to play in college, to play well enough to get drafted into the National Football League, to play in the NFL (not sit on the bench), to be a part of a very good team, to win games inch by inch, yard by yard, year-in and year-out, to win a division, and to go to the big game, and then, to win it. More than once. Not-so-tiny goals, all leading to the big dream.

Not every professional football player makes the playoffs. A professional football player can have a successful—a highly successful—career without ever once playing in the Super Bowl. But if that player retires before he gets the chance to play in the biggest game of all, he will know he never did quite achieve his dream. (I think this is why so many players try to become coaches. They might not get to the big game as a player, but they want to try as a coach.)

A goal is "something somebody wants to achieve." It's "the end of a race." Goals, in some ways, are the opposite of dreams. If you set your goals too high, you'll get discouraged and quit. If you set your dreams too low, you'll get discouraged and quit.

So, how do you set goals? You start with easily achievable ones. The best diet programs are set up this way. They don't put you on a starvation diet of 800 calories per day. If you've been eating 4000 calories per day, the diet will reduce your intake to 3500 calories per day. Most people can easily cut 500 calories from their diet. That's one giant soda or one huge specialty coffee drink or one piece of pie with ice cream. As time goes on, the calorie count goes down incrementally. And the dieter achieves other goals—losing a pound here, fitting into her "skinny" jeans for the first time in years, getting compliments from friends on how good she looks.

However, you can't stop with the small goals. When you achieve a goal, another needs to take its place. Each goal should be a little more difficult than the last. It's like running a marathon: No one can walk out the front door and run 26.2 miles without training. No one, not even the best athletes in the world.

Most people have to walk before they run, and some people can't even walk an entire block without getting winded. Yet within two years, they're able to run 26.2 miles. They didn't increase their distance every day. They walked for a block until they weren't winded. Then they walked for two. Then three. Eventually, they walked for a few blocks and ran for 100 feet. And on and on.

The other key to following goals is to write them down. First, you need to write down what the goal is. Then, you need to keep a log, one that records your struggles to achieve that goal. You will fail. Be honest about those failures. Then, get back up and try again, until you achieve the goal.

Sometimes, the failures tell you that the early goals are too hard. If so, cut the effort in half, and try again.

The other thing you need is a timetable. Give yourself a realistic amount of time to achieve a goal. Once that goal is achieved, have the next goal ready to go, along with its timetable. This is why I tell you to have daily, weekly, monthly, and yearly goals.

Throw in five-year and ten-year goals, as well.

Then, revamp them often. Preferably on a monthly basis. As you strive to achieve those goals, you will learn what is realistic *for you*. No excuses. You need to be one hundred percent honest about what you're trying to do.

If you're an underachiever, pay attention to how hard you work. Make sure you're putting in some real effort and not just slacking off.

If you're an overachiever, make sure you don't work too hard.

That last piece of advice comes from me, the woman who now runs about fifteen miles per week. When I started out, I didn't pay attention to my limits (yes, overachiever), and I achieved…a stress fracture in my foot. Which would have only been a sore foot if I hadn't been so focused on trying to keep up to the impossible goals I had set myself. It would have become a permanently damaged foot if my husband, the former professional athlete, hadn't had a long talk with me about knowing my own limitations (and who also dragged me to the doctor).

It's hard to find a balance between working too hard on your goals and not working hard enough. Which is why I tell you to reassess often. And to be honest with yourself. Because you're the only one who is going to know if you're trying too hard or not trying hard enough.

The goals are stepping stones to that impossible dream. They're the trail through the murk that will lead you to the city on the hill.

They're also the reality check. Because the farther you get down the road, the more you should reassess. You might not want to go to that city on the hill. You might want to jettison your impossible dream because it's not something you want to do any longer.

If that's the case, then you need to find a new dream, or you will stop striving.

I know, I know, I'm speaking in metaphor here. Let me be concrete. One of my early impossible writing goals was to have a career like that of Nora Roberts. But the deeper I got into the writing profession, the more I realized that Nora Roberts and I are very different writers. I would love to have that many bestsellers and all the perks that go with it.

But Nora, for the most part, has stayed within the same genre. She writes all aspects of that genre—romantic suspense, paranormal romance, contemporary romance, even science fiction mystery romance. But the books all center on a couple, either falling in love or striving to maintain their love.

I have a hummingbird brain. I can't even read one genre for longer than a week. Asking me to write in one genre for the rest of my life would actually be a hardship.

As soon as I realized that, I had to look for a new impossible dream. Which was harder than it sounds. Not many writers write in more than one genre. I had to refine the dream to be something that suited me. I've refined several times since then. I still have impossible dreams—but none of them entail writing in the same genre book after book after book.

I reassessed.

If I had wanted a career similar to Nora Roberts's career, I would have had to change my goals. I would have had to write novels in only one genre (although I could've branched into all the subgenres), and I would've had to have small goals along the way—writing a contemporary, writing a paranormal (oh, I've done that), writing a romantic suspense novel (I've done that too!), writing a historical....

You get the picture. My imagination is too dark to sustain a happily-ever-after ending book after book. My sense of whimsy is too powerful to write dark novels book after book. My mind sees too many future possibilities to keep me out of science fiction for too long. But I love to dig deeply into the modern world as well.

I'm not suited for the first city on the hill that I headed toward. However, I've found others that suit me better.

If you think of goals as markers along the way toward your impossible dream, then you've got the right philosophy. If you confuse goals with dreams, then you're going to get stuck.

Imagine something grand for yourself.

Then figure out how to achieve it. If achieving it takes only hard work—if there isn't a little bit of luck and timing involved—then you haven't found your impossible dream yet. Because an impossible dream should have an element of the impossible to it. An element of being in the right place at the right time.

Know too, that you might never achieve that dream—and that's okay. Because you're going to be disappointed when you get to that city. It'll never ever measure up to your imagination. So, as you're on the final road toward your dream, make sure there's a new one waiting in the wings.

And then plan those stepping stones that will get you to your next city on the hill. Set your goals.

Goals are the only thing that will lead to your dream. All of your dreams.

Even those that might never come true.

Patience

Full disclosure time: I have no patience. Or very little patience. I do a good imitation of a person with patience in public, but in my everyday life, I have no idea why everything I want isn't here the moment I want it.

I do understand the irony of me writing a section of the *Guide* on patience, but as someone who lacks something but still desires it, I have made a study of patience.

Patience is essential to building a business, any business. You must do things methodically. You must do them in a particular order, and even then, you might not get an immediate response.

This last bit is a particularly difficult part of owning your own business. We believe that when we put our ads out there, launch our websites, mail our stories or open our shop's door, people will flock in. We'll get an immediate response.

Often, we get no response at all—at least initially. And sometimes, the only response we get is negative.

All of which we should expect—and plan for. But that doesn't make it easy. Nor does it become any easier with time.

Every year, my alma mater, Beloit College, puts out its freshman survey. Someone polls the incoming class about various things—mostly trends—and Beloit publishes the results.

The Class of 2009, born in 1991, is Internet savvy, educated, and informed, but the one thing they lack, according to a former professor of mine, Tom McBride, is patience. This group of kids always got what they wanted when they wanted it. Not just things, but television programs, music, text—all at the touch of a finger.

They haven't learned how to delay gratification—and delayed gratification is what building a business is all about. (You can find 2009's results here.)

I can handle some forms of delayed gratification. I learned way back when that the process is the important thing, not the result. So with that lesson came another: I learned that I had to enjoy the actual work. If I didn't enjoy the work, then I couldn't wait for the result.

This is where my lack of patience works against me. I can wait two weeks or a month or even three months for a check if I enjoyed the work I did to get that check. If I loathe the job, then I want the money immediately. If I don't get the money immediately, I don't do any more work. This is why I'm unemployable on the corporate level.

A business—any business—has good and bad days, fun and difficult work. Early in the life of the business, very little positive happens. You set up systems, establish an office or a storefront, hire a few employees (or not), take out ads (or not), make products and hope they'll sell. You need to get the word out that you are there, wherever there is, and you're ready to do some work for someone.

Then, when you do work for a few someones, you hope they like it enough to recommend you to someone else. In addition to building your office (or your store or your craft), you're building your reputation, good and bad.

You're also building your bank account. In the early days of the business, you're depleting the money you had saved to start the business. If you hadn't saved any money, you're depleting the loan someone (a friend or a financial institution) gave you. As I mentioned before, money goes out the door every single day, but early on, money rarely comes back in.

Goals & Dreams

The early years of a business are all about patience, the early years of a freelance business even more so. You have to be patient as you learn your craft. You have to be patient as you save money to finance the start-up. You have to be patient as you work that day job while you're trying to build a nest egg. You have to be patient as you line up clients, expertise, product.

You have to be so patient that at times it feels like you are doing nothing but being patient.

It's tough, especially in our have-it-now society.

Personally—and this is a bit of an aside—I think one of the good things about the current recession is that people are relearning (or in the case of the 20-somethings, learning) how to wait for something they want. Credit has become tougher to get, so you can't just charge whatever you want even if you can't afford it. Layaway is back. (I hadn't realized it had gone away.) Layaway teaches the value of paying for something without having that something until the money is all in.

In some ways, layaway is what happens as you start a business. You're laying away bits of money, bits of expertise, bits of knowledge, as you prepare for the entire product—which is the ultimate dream.

But patience isn't just essential as you start a business. It's essential to maintaining one.

I'm watching a friend do something fascinating. He has completely abandoned the regular publishing model because its difficulties and slowness drive him crazy and is beginning to self-publish his work electronically. Unfortunately, he hasn't planned for the transition. He doesn't have money saved so that he can contribute to the household, nor does he know how much money he'll actually make on the self-published items.

It's a bold experiment, but he's doing it as a reaction to the things he doesn't like about the existing business he has chosen to participate in, not as a studied, planned expansion of the business he has freelanced in for decades.

If he's lucky, this experiment will work for him. But if the experiment goes as I think it will, he would have been better off working the system he already knew.

Part of the problem is that he's impatient to join the brave new world of electronic publishing. He's jumping in with both feet, without doing any of the due diligence that a wise business owner would do.

The world of electronic publishing is new, and it does require a certain amount of faith. But so does all small business, and there are ways to mitigate potential problems that come from the unknown. I've discussed some of that in previous posts, and I'll discuss more in future posts.

But for the moment, let's stay focused on the issue of patience. How do I, a person with no patience, thrive in a business that requires extreme patience?

I gave you a hint, above.

First, I enjoy the process. I love the work itself. If we got zapped back to the dark ages tomorrow and publishing as we know it disappeared, I'd still write stories on any scrap of paper I could find. I love to write, and that won't change.

(I seriously do not understand writers who say they hate to write but love having written. That makes my brain hurt every time. If you don't like what you do, then why do it? There are easier ways to make a living than writing.)

In fact, for me, the process is why I'm in the writing business. I like everything about writing: I like telling stories. I like playing with words. I like research. I like being alone. I like spending my time in made-up worlds.

I also like the process of freelancing. I'm a bad employee. I hate rules and strictures. I prefer to do things my way in my time, which makes me the quintessential freelancer.

I like being in control of my own destiny. I like the fact that if I don't produce, I don't get paid. I actually hate the idea of going to a job, sitting at a desk, and twiddling my thumbs while I waited for someone to tell me what to do—all for the sake of a paycheck. If you look at my history, you'll realize that I lasted a grand total of three months in every job like that I took. (And I only made it three months because that's about as long as it took me to read every scrap of paper in a normal office.)

But there are many aspects of being my own boss that I don't like. Unfortunately, most of those aspects are essential to the business's survival. I have to mail my work. I have to pay the bills. I have to dun the occasional client for payment. I have to troll for new work. And I have to learn new methods of making money in new mediums or new venues.

How do I handle those things?

Several ways.

I plan. That sounds both silly and essential. Of course, I plan. Every business owner should plan. But as I pointed out above, with the example of my friend, most freelancers don't plan at all. They run after the newest, hottest, shiniest thing. Or they get rid of what's already working because it makes them uncomfortable in order to try something new because it looks easier.

I research heavily, and then I lay out a potential schedule. I make educated guesses about how long it will take me to learn something or incorporate something or change something.

Then I write that plan down step-by-step in my calendar. As I complete each step, I check it off. If the step is particularly difficult, I reward myself with an afternoon off or an ice cream cone or a very noticeable pat on the back. After I've checked that step off, I make sure I'm still on track. If I've learned something that changes the schedule, I make the changes before I move to the next step.

Again, I'm elevating the process into its own little returns-and-reward system. Dean does the same thing, only using his white boards. He makes his lists (charts, actually, for him) in erasable ink. Then, as he completes a step, he either marks down the date or erases the step. He can monitor his progress in that way.

Rather than seeing the task—whatever it is—as one big, difficult, long, torturous thing to complete, I make it a series of smaller tasks, all of them easy to complete. That helps with my impatience because I don't have to wait six months for results. I get results every week or sometimes every single day.

I only schedule things that I control. For example, when you open a store, you can't say with any certainty when the first customer will walk through the door. All you can do is plan for the moment the store is ready for business.

In publishing, I can't control when someone will buy something. I can only write to the best of my ability and have a lot of product in the mail to people who might buy it. There are three factors at work here: the product has to be good, there has to be a lot of it, and it has to be in front of someone who will consider it for publication. I can control all three of those things.

So I don't plan to have sold something by January 1. Instead, I plan to have five short stories done and mailed by that date. And then I move to the next date, and the date after that.

If I work on the things I can control, things that I know will improve my business, then the goodness will follow.

A note here: I have noticed that good things come in waves. In publishing, sales come in waves. As do good reviews or award nominations. This also happens in retail. A store will have several good days in a row, with a lot of customers and sales, followed by weeks of slow days or days with no customers at all. And the irritating thing about this is that the ups and downs are impossible to predict.

So, if you're always waiting for someone else to do something, then you'll run out of patience quickly. But if you do the things that you can control, then you're going to be too busy to notice what that someone else is doing—and when they finally get to it, you'll be taken by surprise.

In this way, my friend's plan to self-publish is a good one. He's taking control of his backlist and his front list.

What he's missing—at least from the outside—is this next thing.

I maintain my base. By this I mean I continue to do the things that allow my business to thrive. I write short stories in part because I love them and in part because I have an audience for them. I resell things I've already published because that's income for very little work on my part. I am constantly looking for new markets so that when the old ones disappear, I still have work.

As I add in new things (such as slowly adding mystery writing to my science fiction writing), I don't abandon what has already worked for me. I research the new markets and slowly put a toe into the water, instead of jumping into the deep end, abandoning my safe spot on the shore.

In other businesses, that's keeping the regular clients while bringing in new clients. Just because one new client promises to give you more work than you can handle doesn't mean you should take on that client. Research first, see if the money is what is promised, see if the client will actually be someone you want to work with (or for), and then slowly bring that client into your business.

Don't let the untested new thing take over because you're impatient for results.

If you're anything like me, telling you to be patient is like waving a red flag in front of a bull. That's guaranteed to make me impatient. But if I have a plan, I can take all the time I need to get where I'm going.

Because I enjoy the journey.

And, ultimately, that's what freelancing is all about. Enjoying the process—and celebrating each positive result.

Expectations

A short time ago, a young writer who did not know my history in the science fiction field mentioned in e-mail how much he hated certain editors. He felt those editors had mislead him and were, therefore, unethical people.

Since those editors happened to be friends of mine of long standing—I'd known both for more than twenty years—I knew they weren't unethical people. Nor would they deliberately mislead writers.

After a few back-and-forths, I found out what happened: those editors had met this young writer in a networking situation (one a convention, the other a guest lecture at a writer's workshop) and invited him to submit stories to their various projects.

The writer had submitted stories, which were then kindly, but soundly, rejected. He was furious. He thought the editors had broken an implied promise. By inviting him to submit—he thought—the editors were committing to buy the stories.

Never mind that neither editor had ever seen his work before. Never mind that they had no idea whether he even wrote in the genre.

He hadn't thought the situation through. A little more probing uncovered something else: he had an improper understanding of the writing field.

Somehow, this young writer had gotten it into his head that most writers sold stories not because the stories were good, but because the writer had met the editor and the editor liked the writer. I have no idea where that idea had come from—it certainly isn't written down anywhere, even as a myth—but it had embedded itself firmly in this writer's brain.

(To clarify, in case any others out there have this notion in their minds: stories sell because the stories are good. There are other factors such as what the publisher wants for the magazine/book line. For example, no matter how excellent a hardboiled mystery is, you won't sell it to a sweet romance book line. It just won't happen.)

Before you sit back smugly and think that you would never make a mistake like the one this young writer made, realize that everyone who is in business for himself—every single freelancer/business owner—has made this mistake at least once. Many make it every single day.

The mistake comes from unrealistic expectations.

I almost wrote that it comes from expectations (leaving out the word "unrealistic"), and although that might be true (we shouldn't have expectations; we should have plans), without some measure of expectation, we probably can't do what we want to do. I'll get to that in a bit. But first, let's deal with unrealistic expectations.

When my ex-husband and I opened our frame shop and art gallery twenty-mumble years ago, my ex was the realist (for once). He knew that he couldn't open the store without a customer base already in place. I was the unrealistic one: I thought that because we had a storefront and a sign above the door and lovely inventory and a talented framer, we would have customers on the very first day we opened. We did, but only because my ex ran his legs off. He planned a grand opening, sent out invitations (with maps), called people, and made sure everyone who needed to know about the store did know. And then he grew the business.

Goals & Dreams

I had *Field of Dreams* in mind: Somehow, I believed if we built it, they would come.

Many retail store owners make that mistake. I just watched the same thing happen this last year. A woman opened a what-not shop in the same local mall as the collectibles store Dean had started. The what-not shop, which this poor woman had spent years saving items and money for, was no different than three similar stores that had not survived in that location, and sadly, her store wasn't as nice as the two other what-not stores that already existed in the same mall.

Anyone with any business experience could have told her the store would fail. She had the wrong location, and she was undercapitalized. She couldn't wait long enough to build a customer base; she didn't even have enough money to join a group ad for the mall in the local paper. When the business went under, after less than a year, none of her neighbors were surprised—and none were sympathetic. Everyone mentioned how unrealistic her expectations were, and one other store owner even mentioned the *Field of Dreams* analogy, albeit in reverse.

"Just because you build it," he said in his curmudgeonly way, "doesn't mean anyone will come."

He was right. It made the loss no less painful for this poor woman. Her dream died in short order. But of all the things she did wrong—and she did quite a few (all first-time business owners and freelancers make horrible mistakes)—the worst thing was the devastation left by her unrealistic expectation.

How can you start a business without expectations? You can't. You have to have expectations of success or there really is no point in going out on your own. How many people do you know who start a business saying that they believe it will fail? I've never met anyone like that.

But your expectations have to be realistic. The woman shop owner hadn't done any research. She had planned and dreamed for her store, but she hadn't researched how to run a business or how much capital she would need. She had assumed these things would come to her.

I dealt with some of this in the section on Goals and Dreams, but expectations are subtler than either of those two things, and they blow up on you when you least expect it.

I had one of those expectation bombs blow up on me this year—and I didn't even see it coming. My twenty-fourth birthday was terrible. I spent the day alone. My friends had moved out of town, my family forgot my birthday, and my ex-husband didn't even remember to get me a cake (yes, I know, the handwriting was on the wall at that point).

I spent the day alone, stuck on the farm that we lived above without a car, so I couldn't even go into town to entertain myself. I read, watched a little television, and generally felt sorry for myself. I also—Scarlett O'Hara-like—vowed I would never have another crappy birthday again, even if I had to make sure the celebrations happened. I promised myself that when I got old and was rich and famous, I would give myself the party of a lifetime. I would pay for all of it—spending tens of thousands of dollars on caterers and airline tickets for all my friends and family—and it would last all weekend, and it would be very, very *Dynasty*, with designer clothes, rich food, and upscale swanky digs.

Fast forward to January 1, 2010. 2010—the year I turned fifty.

I had a complete and utter meltdown. Not because I turned fifty. But because—apparently—to the 24-year-old me, 50 is really, really old.

The expectation bomb went off. My 24-year old self had planted a huge landmine and as the calendar turned to 2010, I stepped on that damn mine. I realized I don't have *Dynasty*-level money. I couldn't afford to fly my friends and family into some swanky resort somewhere and spend what would have been in 1984 dollars tens of thousands of dollars but what is in 2010 dollars hundreds of thousands of dollars on a party. I don't have hundreds of thousands of dollars lying around—and if I did, I'd pay off my house and add to my savings, not spend every last dime on designer duds for my shindig.

I knew that. Realistically, I should have shrugged and laughed at my 24-year-old self. But built into that party expectation were two other expectations. The first expectation was that fifty was really, really, really old. I became ancient—at least to that poor lonely girl I had once been. And second—I should be a multimillionaire, maybe even a billionaire, by now. I should have a household name like Stephen King or Nora Roberts or J.K. Rowling.

I don't.

So—by the lights of the expectation bomb I planted at the ripe old age of 24—I am both old *and* a failure.

Oh, and happy 50th birthday!

Ouch, ouch, ouch.

I've run into a million of those personal expectation bombs throughout my career. Some are pretty easy to see—if I sell my first short story, I'll have it made. If I sell my first novel, I'll be rich. But others aren't visible until you step on them (which is why I'm using the term landmine). When I got nominated for my first Edgar award (and typing that phrase is a trip, even now—my *first* Edgar), I almost declined it but I managed to stop myself just in time.

When Dean asked why I would do such a thing, I heard myself answer, "Because I'm not good enough to be nominated for an Edgar." It took some digging to find when I planted that particular landmine. I had planted it (we plant all these expectation landmines) during the summers of my childhood, then continued to grow the mine during my adulthood, by buying novels with Edgar-winner emblazoned on them. I had used "Edgar-winner" as a stamp of quality—and it is a tribute to that award that I was rarely, if ever, disappointed.

Instead of being flattered and honored at first, I was terrified that I had been nominated by accident.

Pieces of that landmine still exist, as you can tell from my parenthetical phrase about my first Edgar award, but now I have that particular bomb under control.

Not all of these landmines are about success. Some are about failure. A pragmatic friend of mine knew the statistics when he started his business. He knew that it took five years to establish most businesses, and since his was particularly tricky, he figured he might not be successful even five years in.

That was his expectation, and his mantra, and he recited it often.

Surprise, surprise: His business got established within two years. He started making a profit. About the time he should have grown the business or made a few changes dictated by his success, he didn't even notice. Instead, he continued to talk about the three more years he had before his business got established.

No amount of arguing could change his mind; he expected to have a rough first five years. He didn't notice the success and actively sabotaged it. By not seeing his situation realistically, he lost his business within six years, and declared himself unsurprised.

What surprised him was that as he put the bank books into storage, he realized that he had achieved his success four years previously. He was stunned. He saw his business through the prism of his unrealistic (negative) expectations, and as a result he made mistakes that caused his business to meet those expectations and fail.

How do you root out these unrealistic expectations?

I wish I knew. I'd do a deep personal inventory of my psyche right now and make all of my unrealistic expectations disappear. In fact, I would have done it years ago, so this past January 1 would have been a pleasant day instead of the nightmare it became, all because I tripped over a mental landmine.

In the 26 years since I planted that particular landmine, however, I have learned how to recognize some of those unrealistic expectations and how to prevent them from becoming time bombs.

1. Don't plant the unrealistic expectation in the first place.

Listen to yourself as you make casual and joking statements. An old friend of mine had a habit that he had to force himself to quit. When a waitress asked, "What would you like?" My friend would say, "I'd like to be rich and never have to work again."

That's a very funny statement—particularly in that context (and with the right waitress who also sees the humor)—but it has an unrealistic expectation built into the middle of the joke. "I'd like to be rich *and never have to work again.*" Most rich people work. The ones who lose their riches let someone else manage their money. Money management *is* work. So, if my friend had become rich before he stopped saying this little bon mot, he would have stopped working, too—and probably would have lost all or most of his money to an unscrupulous money manager.

2. Research your expectations.

Has anyone become rich and never had to work again? If so, how? And if not, why not? And really—this one was always the key for me when my friend made his little joke—do you want to stop working? I know a lot of fantastically wealthy people who still work. They work harder than everyone else *because they enjoy their jobs.*

I'm sure Steven Spielberg could have stopped working somewhere around 1980, but luckily for modern American film he did not. Stephen King could have stopped writing about the same time. As a fan, I'm happy he didn't.

If I had *Dynasty*-level money and could have thrown myself that party this year, I would still be working. I love what I do. The money isn't the reward; it's a byproduct of being able to do what I love.

3. Research everything.

Before you go into business for yourself, research the industry. Then research money management. Then research business. Listen to the negatives and the positives. If you don't like what you hear, figure out how you can avoid those problems.

If someone tells you that no one succeeds in your industry (writers hear this all the time), investigate. See if that's true. See if you can find five people who succeeded in your industry. Then ten. Then twenty.

If someone tells you there's only one way to succeed, see if that's true. Usually it isn't. Ask questions. Find the answers. And don't take the first answer. Get a second, third, and fourth opinion.

4. Research continually.

Make sure you keep up with your industry. If your freelancing business is in trouble, figure out why. Make the necessary changes to save it. Then make sure you do enough research so that you won't make that same mistake again.

5. Listen to people who are already successful in your field.

Those people will often offer you advice, but that advice might be oblique. I can't tell you how many times early in my writing career a very successful writer would say in the middle of a conversation, "That attitude will get you in trouble."

I would be defensive, or I would ignore the sentence. I'd rarely follow up. But years later, I would remember the comment when that attitude—in the form of an unrealistic expectation—*did* get me in trouble. And sometimes, I was lucky enough to have the opportunity to go back to that writer and ask how to repair the damage caused by that expectation landmine.

Nowadays, however, I'm often the writer who says, "That attitude will get you in trouble," and I watch as writer after writer ignores me. Early on, a writer friend (and former student of mine) was making such an egregious error, based on an unrealistic expectation, that I actually told him point-by-point why he should not take that terrible action. He got angry and defensive and then told me I had no idea what I was talking about.

At that moment, I realized why the sentence "That attitude will get you into trouble," gets spoken, but no successful person ever follows up on it unless asked to. The newer professional has to want the information and has to be willing to hear the answer.

6. Pay attention to the questions you can't answer.

These are tough. They're the kind of questions that, if your parents had asked them when you were a kid, you probably would have answered like this: *My friends are doing it.* And if your parents were like mine, they'd haul out the old *If your friends were jumping off a cliff, would you follow?*

You'll probably have elaborate justifications built up in your mind, and you'll offer them as answers to the question. But listen to that whisper, which happens just before you offer up the first justification.

For example (and I'm clearly making this up):
Question: Why do you need ten $250,000 cars?
Justification: I collect them.

The Whispered Thought: Rich people own dozens of outrageously expensive cars, and now that I'm rich, I need to *act* rich.

Each business has those same unrealistic expectations built in. A writer friend of mine rented an office outside the house because (justification) he "needed quiet to work." Real reason? He believed that people who worked at home were not working, even though he had made 50K a year while working at home. (The office ate up his profits, and he eventually moved back home to save money—and in the process had to ferret out the unreasonable expectation that had caused the problem in the first place.)

An acquaintance of mine graduated from law school in the middle of her class. The law school was the best in her state and in the state's major city. However, that city was overrun with graduates from the law school, most of whom graduated with a better record than she had. When she couldn't get a job in any of the city's law firms (not a one) because her grades were not as good as other applicants, she didn't move to a different city. Nor did she do some volunteer lawyering or take a job at Legal Aid, like some of my other friends who had not graduated at the top of their class.

Instead, she hung out her own shingle in a town filled with lawyers. She got a few clients—not enough to pay the bills—and because she thought she only needed the law degree, not actually do any hard work, she did a poor job.

Why would this bright woman believe that she could survive in the cutthroat legal atmosphere of the state's major city with just a law degree?

Her justification was that no law firm hired women like her— which was true in the year she was born. But in the 1990s, when she was trying to do this, law firms hired women all the time.

The whispered unrealistic expectation? Real lawyers worked for a law firm. If no firm would hire her, she had to set up her own firm. She didn't believe real lawyers worked for Legal Aid or as legislative counsel to a state senator or as in-house attorney at some corporation.

Her law firm—and eventually her dream of being a lawyer— disappeared under the weight of her unrealistic expectation.

7. If people tell you you're acting irrationally given the evidence around you or events around you, check to see if you're acting out of an unrealistic expectation.

Think back to my successful friend who refused to believe his business had become successful after two years (when he expected it to take five). From the moment he refused to believe his business was doing better than most, many of his actions were irrational— and people told him so. If he had analyzed the comments and done a little research, he might have saved that business.

But he attributed them all to jealousy or to other motives on the part of the other people. Granted, people will tell you things out of fear or jealousy. That's why I tell you to research their comments. See if their statements are true. If not, dismiss them. If so, pay attention—and maybe make some changes.

We all have unrealistic expectations about ourselves, our careers, and our birthdays. (Well, maybe I'm the only one with an unrealistic expectation about a birthday.) These unrealistic expectations can ruin our careers—either by giving us the wrong benchmarks (why does anyone need a *Dynasty*-style party at any age?) or by making us refuse to see what we really have.

You'll never find all of your unrealistic expectations. But you'll track down some of the important ones. And if you do, you'll stop tripping over landmines and start walking forward, which, after all, is how every business progresses. One not-always-smooth step at a time.

Giving Up On Yourself

Amazing the difference eighteen months make. I first wrote the posts entitled "Giving Up On Yourself (Parts One and Two)" in June of 2010. But as we head into 2012, I realize that some of what I wrote is out of date.

I've revised this section. The core information is the same but the outdated information is now gone. I initially wrote this section about giving up on yourself by focusing on publishing. But I no longer agree with those parts of the section. I am going to keep the overall structure, talking about artists first. So, the initial introduction is gone, but the important stuff remains.

KKR,
November 2011

First, a disclaimer. The *Freelancer's Survival Guide* is for freelancers of all stripes, not just writers, actors, musicians and people who work in the arts. The *Guide* is for anyone who works for herself.

This topic applies to all of us, but I'm going to start with artists —and by that I mean people who make their living in the arts— before I broaden the scope of the topic.

Artists occupy a rather unique place in the freelance firmament. Unlike most professionals, artists don't need a formal education. Artists don't need a license to hang out a shingle. Anyone can declare himself an artist, quit his day job, and try to make a living from his work.

While that's sometimes freeing, it's also a danger. Because unlike a doctor who can't get his license without years of formal training and a certain level of competency, an artist can start "working" the moment she sings her first note or draws her first straight line. In some professions (the securities trade comes to mind), this level of accepted incompetence gives rise to fraud. In the arts, however, the only person who gets cheated when an artist is inexperienced is the artist herself.

Most people who attempt a career in the arts suffer from a mixture of extreme ego and extreme insecurity. We need the extreme ego to attempt success on an international level. After all, what makes our voices different from everyone else's? There are billions of people on the Earth. Why do we believe that we will stand out?

Ego gives us that belief. But common sense tells us that we will fail at our goal. Worse, we take every mistake to heart. Most artists are sensitive souls, easily wounded by criticism. We believe in ourselves, but not all the time. That insecurity keeps us grounded. It also gives us an Achilles heel.

When the ego and the insecurity are out of balance, the artist tips in the wrong direction. Too much ego and the artist becomes insufferable. A mild-mannered bookstore owner once told me the story of the one and only time he kicked an author out of his store. The author was doing a book signing. A line of customers waited there to get their books autographed. The author was so abusive to his fans, he reduced even the most jaded of them to tears. The bookstore owner stepped in, stopped the signing, and when the author got more belligerent, asked the author to leave. The author refused, the owner threatened to call the police, and the author left in a storm of invective.

That author's ego was so out of control that he alienated

everyone around him. In fact, when the bookstore owner told me who the author was, I was not surprised. I had heard through other sources what a mean, egotistical jerk this man was.

At the time of the signing debacle, the author had several books on the *New York Times* Bestseller List. Now, no major publishing house will touch him. Why? His ego. His writing is just as good as it always was, maybe better. But no one in a major publishing house—from the publisher to the editor to the sales force—wants to deal with the man. He has alienated everyone in the business.

An out-of-control ego is one side of the imbalance. The other side is rampant insecurity. I can tell you of writer after writer—many of them former students of mine—who write tremendous fiction and can't sell a word. Why? Because they refuse to let the work leave their offices, believing it no good. A single negative comment will get them to shelve not just that work, but also any other work that might be in the same genre or have the same tone.

I threaten a few of them occasionally, saying I'll go into their files and mail their stories for them, but, of course, I don't follow through. Because Dean and I have a philosophy that runs through all of our workshops:

You Are Responsible For Your Own Career

The egomaniacal writer I mentioned above is responsible for the downturn in his career. The insecure writers I mentioned right after him are responsible for the fact that most readers have never heard of them.

Artists must learn to balance that insecurity and ego so that they're not raving lunatics (except in the privacy of their own offices) and so that they're not so self-effacing that they refuse to let their brilliant work see the light of day.

Successful artists walk that line every single day. Push any of us hard enough in either direction and you'll hear a burst of ego or a whisper of insecurity. But neither will last long, and one (the ego) will often result in an immediate apology.

No successful artist has gotten where she is without paying her dues. Paying dues is a long, hard slog, often done in complete solitude. The end result is rather like the end result of going to medical school. You emerge exhausted, different, but with a working knowledge of your field and yourself. You must continue learning from that point on, constantly improving your craft, or you will destroy something (or someone—including, but not limited to, yourself).

When I started in the writing profession, paying dues took a certain amount of courage as well as ego. Most writers did not live anywhere near publishing central, which was (at least for Americans) New York City. We had to convince someone we'd never met to buy our work, and we had to do it via snail mail. Cold-calling an editor was a breach of etiquette. So was dropping into an editor's office if, indeed, you decided to fly yourself to New York. Writers' conferences were few and far between.

You had only yourself, your words, and your trusty (but somewhat inaccurate and out-of-date) *Writer's Market*. You had to take the flyer.

It took years to run that gauntlet, often with little or no feedback. The writers who survived the constant rejection, the writers who worked at improving each and every day, the writers who *persisted* against all odds, became the ones whose names you recognize now.

All of the arts had some form of this gauntlet: musicians made demo tapes that had to be mailed to various record studios; artists developed portfolios that had to be mailed to galleries or publishing houses; actors sent resumes and photographs before getting auditions. We didn't have the benefit of the Internet. We couldn't build websites that promoted our work, and we couldn't tell someone to look at our online résumé/portfolio/demo.

I'm excited about the changes digital media will bring to my industry. I already love the way that it has changed the other arts. I can now look at my favorite artists' portfolios online or listen to music from musicians who don't get Top 40 airplay. I watch made-for-internet-only video, and I spend too much time looking for the unknown on the web.

But I worry. I watch the Internet providing newer artists with an easy way to give up on themselves.

I see this most strongly in the publishing industry because that's where I'm tapped in. Instead of a writer enduring years of rejection to get a book published, learning craft, improving, figuring out how to entice a publisher to buy the work (learning the proper use of an agent—which is not as a publisher's first reader), learning the entire business as she gains experience, writers now make a few attempts and then give up.

Initially, when I wrote this piece, I said that new writers who didn't try the traditional publishing gauntlet were giving up on themselves. At the time—eighteen months ago—I was on the cusp of being wrong. I hadn't seen the changes in the industry or if I had seen them, I hadn't understood them.

Back then—and before—it was easy to see a writer who was giving up on herself. She tossed in the towel, didn't fight that gauntlet, and just defaulted with publishing online.

Now it could be argued—and I just might do it some day—that writers who refuse to learn how to publish their own work (particularly their backlist, if they're professional writers) are giving up on themselves. These writers don't have to do the work themselves, but they should learn how to hire the best help *for a flat fee*, and then get that work online.

Because, in just the eighteen months since I originally wrote this piece, e-books have become 25% of the book market (and they'll continue to grow), bookstores have all but vanished except in a few (lucky) places, and most books are ordered online. There is now little that a traditional publisher can do that a writer can't do herself —provided she's willing to learn how.

The learning is the key. Because the writer who gives up on himself is the writer who stops learning.

There are a variety of ways to see that unwillingness to learn.

Among professionals, it's a refusal to look at the changes in the industry and figure out how to apply those changes to the writer's advantage. The writer remains stuck in the old way of doing things and never even bothers to look at the new way.

Among newcomers, it's an unwillingness to admit that they still have learning to do in their craft. Maybe their self-published title isn't selling because it's unusual. But maybe it's not selling because readers have sampled it and found it lacking—either in storytelling, grammatical basics, or in just plain old good writing.

The publishing craft might be lacking, as well. The writer might have a great story buried in terrible formatting, hidden behind an awful cover, or hidden behind a bad cover blurb. All of these are skills that a writer can learn or, if he has the funds, he can hire someone to do the work for him *for a flat fee*.

I keep repeating that flat fee statement because yet another way for writers to give up on themselves is to fail to understand business. Right now, writers can post their work online or do the work to do a trade paper edition, and get up to 70% of the profits. But so many writers are refusing to learn the various ways to do this and retain that 70% profit. Writers can retain the profit either by learning to do the work themselves or paying someone *a flat fee* to do the work for them.

Too many writers—most of them, in fact—are paying some "professional" as much as 50% of that 70% to do the work for them. Work that will take the "professional" a few hours, and that professional will keep earning a profit on that work for years, maybe even decades.

The difference here is that the writer hasn't learned business, and refuses to. He's giving up on himself and in doing so is costing himself thousands, maybe hundreds of thousands, of dollars over decades.

That frustrates me to no end.

Musicians, who've been struggling with this ten years longer than writers, have learned to have multiple platforms. They make sure their music is available in vinyl, CD, and MP3. They license usage rights to radio stations as well as television shows and commercials. They do more concerts than they used to, just to get the music heard. The big recording studios still exist, but they are more selective than ever about the artists they back. The difference is that the artists who have a shot at the bigs and fail to achieve a studio's numbers now have something to fall back on, and a way to rebuild.

Actors no longer have to choose between stage, screen, and small screen. They work in short video, live-action films, YouTube stories. They work on basic cable and premium channel films. They take television shows, even though that would have been the kiss of death to a movie career twenty years ago, and they do a lot of international work. The markets, in all of the arts, are changing.

But the changing markets shouldn't be an excuse for failing to try hard. It's pretty easy to see why an actor isn't getting work if he posts his latest homemade video on YouTube and it's filled with too much emoting and not enough emotion. Anyone can spend days watching singers on YouTube attempting to become the next Justin Bieber. Most of those singers are out of tune and have no performance skills at all. It's hard to become a professional musician. You need a certain level of skill, not just a pleasant voice.

Sadly, it's the same for writers. You need a certain level of skill to succeed on an international level, and now, the only way to know if you have that skill is to trust the readers. The readers will find your work. If it's good, it'll sell—not at huge numbers per month, but a few copies here and there. If the sales remain consistent or grow, you're doing a good job. If you sell five copies in July of 2012 and only one copy in the next six months, then there might be something wrong with the product.

Should you figure out what that something is? Should you rewrite the book to death? Heck, no. You should practice—keep writing *new* material, and learn, learn, learn. After a few years, come back to the book that's not selling. You will see it differently. You will know if the cover is bad or the blurb fails. You'll know if there is no opening hook.

Provided you've been learning and growing and getting better.

All freelancers succeed because they persist. They try, they fail, they learn. They try again, they fail, they learn. They keep trying, keep learning, until they get a glimmer of success. Success rarely comes overnight. It comes after years of hard and often thankless work.

People who go into business for themselves expecting it to be easy are bound to fail, and fail in a spectacular way. Working for yourself is hard. You have a lot of decisions to make, a lot of assessing to do.

How does all of this publishing/artist talk apply to those of you who don't work in the arts? Simple, really. There are things that you can do for your business that look like get-rich-quick short cuts. You've probably tried them. You know that they don't work.

What works is learning the ropes and becoming the best at what you do.

Sometimes that means going out on a limb with a project no one else believes in. But if it's early in your career and no one has believed in you yet, then perhaps the problem isn't that the project is too new or too innovative or too different for other people to appreciate.

Maybe the problem is that you haven't learned your craft yet. You don't know how to run the most efficient business possible. You haven't learned the tricks of your trade.

When you always take the easy route, you're giving up on yourself. Take that ego of yours and remind it that you need to be the *best* at what you do. And the best never takes the easy route.

Then take that insecurity of yours and tell it that you need to work harder to get better. It'll take over from there. And it'll balance out the ego that seems to think it should be rewarded just for trying.

I know. I know. It's not always easy versus hard. The answers aren't always clear-cut. How do you know when you're giving up on yourself versus being innovative? What if there's no clear path?

I also know that it's different for other types of freelancers. The digital world isn't one-type-fits-all. For example, retail stores with unique inventories are actually hurting themselves if they don't have

Goals & Dreams

a significant online presence. Same with real estate agencies. Doctors are starting to investigate the benefits of e-mail "appointments" for minor matters. Every type of business is different.

So if they're all different, then how do you figure out where you stand? Are you working hard enough? Are you giving yourself enough credit? Are you hurting or helping yourself?

How do you know if you're giving up on yourself?

First, recognize that giving up on yourself isn't black and white. Just because something is easy doesn't make it wrong. Just because something is hard doesn't make it right. To know if you're giving up on yourself, you first have to figure out who you are.

Oh, yeah, that's simple. Take a lifelong task and figure it out in the next twenty minutes. Not.

What I mean by that is this:

Figure out what your dreams are. Write them down. Figure out what your goals are. Write them down.

Once you've figured out what your dreams and goals are *today, right now, this instant*, honestly assess if you're on the right road to attaining those dreams and goals. Only you know what your dreams and goals are and whether you're really on the right path to achieving those dreams and goals.

I stress that only you can figure out if you're on the right path because sometimes—to an outsider—it looks like you've given up on yourself when you really haven't.

For example, my husband has a degree in architecture and three years of law school. He quit in the last week of his last semester of law school because he realized he did not want to be a lawyer, and if he had graduated from the University of Idaho Law School, he would automatically have had most of the responsibilities of a lawyer, even if he never wanted to practice law.

So, one week before graduation, he became a full-time bartender and school bus driver. To anyone looking at him from the outside, it would seem like he had given up on himself.

Instead, he focused on his writing career. Becoming a full-time professional writer isn't something you can do overnight. It takes years, and he had just embarked on that career. But think about it from the point of view of his friends and family: he was a thirty-something former professional golfer and professional skier, who had given up "guaranteed" careers in architecture and the law, to what? Spend all his time in bars? Noodle on his computer?

It seemed like he had given up on himself when, for maybe the first time in his life, he had actually started to take himself seriously. Now he's a bestselling writer, with more than ninety novels published. In hindsight, he made the right—the obvious—decision. But only in hindsight.

What did Dean have that many people do not have? He had a firm belief in himself and a willingness to take risks to achieve his goals. Those risks often made him go against common wisdom, and to fight against the beliefs of others.

That's tough. But that's what people with non-traditional professions, freelancers in other words, have to do.

So, how do freelancers know when they're giving up on themselves?

Here's where it gets tough, because sometimes (often!) the act of giving up on yourself is by degrees. It's subtle. It's settling for a little less than you want. It's slowly moving off the path until one day you wake up and realize that not only have you left the path you wanted to walk but you're also not even going in the right direction any more. And you got there by varying your course by half-inches instead of making hard right turns. Sometimes you didn't even notice as you went off course.

To keep from giving up on yourself, you must:

1. Believe in yourself.

I know, I know. You're insecure. You're uncertain. We *all* are. And sometimes, articulating those big dreams out loud just sounds ridiculous, especially if you haven't had any achievements in your field yet.

So, how do you gain a belief in yourself when you really have none? I take a tip from the training that actors receive. Pretend. Pretend you have the belief. *Act* as if you do. Figure out how people who believe in themselves would act in that situation, and then mimic them. Eventually, it will become habit. And somewhere along the way, you will realize that you actually do believe in yourself. To be otherwise would feel odd.

2. Stop the negative self-talk.

If you hear yourself saying, "I'll never be able to do that," add "if I don't try." Give yourself little pep talks. Keep your focus on what you can control. Remember that your goal is a hard one and will take a lot of effort. So, reward yourself for the small steps.

A corollary to this is: stop talking to/listening to the negative people around you. For every person who thinks something will work, there are five who will tell you the flaws in your plan. First, look at the source. If the person who tells you the flaws hasn't done anything with his own life, realize that what he's telling you is what goes on in his head every single day. Those negative words are the ones he lives with and the ones that have prevented him from achieving his dreams. He thinks he's being helpful. And he is. He's giving you an example of where you'll be if you listen to him.

You can cut the negative people out of your life, but that isn't always productive. I have some marvelous friends who can be very negative about any dreams or goals. I just don't discuss my future plans with those people. (I often don't mention my successes to them, either.) I enjoy their company on a casual level, and I keep the relationship on that level.

3. Perform a daily gut check.

Make sure you're on the right path each and every day. Seriously. Your gut will twist slightly if you're making a poor decision. That feeling is different from the feeling you get when you make a risky-but-good decision.

Let's see if I can describe the difference. If you're making a risky-but-good decision, you'll feel a bit lightheaded, a bit breathless, and a little frightened. You know it can go wrong, but you're willing to risk it.

If you're making a mistake, veering ever so slightly off the road toward your dreams, you might feel lightheaded and frightened, but you'll also feel just a little sick. Often, if you're paying attention to that voice inside your head, the one that gives you advice (good and bad), you'll hear it say, *"That's okay. I'll be all right. I can live with that."*

4. Watch out for that evil phrase, "I can live with that."

"I can live with that," is often accompanied by "for a few weeks, for a year." But add "forever" to that phrase. Can you live with it now? Can you live with it forever, if you know it means you'll never achieve your dream?

Sometimes, you have to live with something. Several of my friends have been taking care of their elderly, very sick parents. My friends have volunteered to live with financial hardship and emotional difficulties so long as their parents are alive. My friends also know that this will lead to some deferred goals. But they're willing to make that choice—and they know, by the very nature of the task they're facing—that they won't have to live in this situation for the rest of their lives.

Dean has a great way of analyzing the "I can live with this" part of life. He asks—quite pointedly—"Do you want to be doing this in one year? In five years? In ten?"

If you answer those questions honestly, you'll know if you're making too many compromises. For example, I would hate to have to go back and wait tables to finance my writing. But I'd do it, if the writing stopped earning money for me. I'd do it for the rest of my life if it meant I could keep writing.

But I wouldn't take on another profession. I never could imagine myself being a news director forever or even a journalist forever. Nor could I imagine myself editing magazines and books for the rest of my life.

While those professions seem close to professional fiction writing, they *aren't* professional fiction writing. In fact, they get in the way of professional fiction writing.

For a while, I was better known as an editor in the field of science fiction and fantasy than I was as a writer. I was an acclaimed, award-winning editor, and if you look at the circulation figures, the years I edited *The Magazine of Fantasy & Science Fiction* were the years of its highest circulation *in its entire existence*. In other words, I was good at my job. Very good.

I liked the job at first, came to hate it by the end. If I had remained as an editor (and I had dozens of editing job offers after I quit; in fact, I still get editing job offers every now and then), I would have been remembered, acclaimed, famous—and I would have given up on myself. At that point in time, most people believed I was a better editor than writer, and that I was making a huge mistake giving up the editing career.

It was one of the best decisions of my life.

But editing was very seductive. It wasn't easier than writing for me. It was harder. I had to work for someone else. I had to fit myself into a mold that wasn't comfortable for me.

However, editing gave me great acclaim and respect. I had achieved, by the age of thirty-five, fame in my chosen genre (science fiction and fantasy) and I was at the pinnacle of my editing career. I could have stayed at that pinnacle for decades, if I had chosen to do so.

It would have been close to a writing career. In fact, it mimicked the writing career in all but the production of stories. I even wrote a lot of words—editorials, interstitial materials, essays. But I didn't write fiction.

I had been writing fiction since I was seven years old. Giving up on fiction for a career in sf would have been giving up on myself.

And yet, waiting tables—even now—wouldn't be. Waiting tables would enable me to concentrate on writing during my off hours. I would put in my time for my paycheck, come home, and do what I love. And that's extremely important to me—more important than being remembered or being the center of a certain genre or being a big shot.

I am a storyteller at heart. And I am happiest when I write down my stories and try to get them published. So long as I do that, I am staying true to myself.

5. Watch out for "good enough."

I hate that phrase, "Good enough." The thing that got me to work hardest on my fiction was a comment Frederick Pohl made about my writing at a writing workshop. He said he would have bought a story of mine—not because it was memorable or brilliant, but because he had a 3,000-word gap in his magazine and my 3,000-word story was *good enough*.

Ack. Kiss of death. I never want to be good enough. I want to be the best.

"Good enough" is settling. And I never want to settle. Not in my fiction ("Oh, my writing is good enough. I don't have to learn any more.") Or in my life ("Oh, this job is good enough. I'll get by.") "Good enough" is as deadly as "I can live with that."

Only, "good enough" crops up in other ways. Like this:

- **I'm good enough to do something as a hobby, but not good enough to do it as a profession.**
- **This is good enough to get by.**
- **I'll never be good enough to achieve my dream.**

All three are deadly thoughts.

Let's take them one at a time. "I'm good enough to do something as a hobby, but not good enough to do it as a profession."

That sentence has a whole bunch of levels. First of all, who decides what "good enough" to do something professionally is?

And let's say there are standards; who says you can't improve? Who says you can't get better?

Why are you afraid to try?

"This is good enough to get by." Why are you settling for "getting by"? Why aren't you striving to do your best?

"I'll never be good enough to achieve my dream." Here's a secret: people who achieve their dreams are never "good enough." They're always trying to get better. In fact, they never believe they have reached a plateau. "Good enough" suggests there is one.

And here's a final one. If you're constantly satisfied with "good enough" in your field of endeavor, ask yourself this: Are you in the right field? Because if you're not willing to constantly improve, if you're willing to settle, then you are not enjoying your work.

There are a bunch of reasons for failing to enjoy your work. You might be burned out. You might be overworked. Or you might not like the work itself.

Many of us have had dreams that have proven wrong for us. I love music, but when it comes to being a musician, I always settle. I never strive. I practice until I'm "good enough" to get by. And no matter what I do, I cannot break myself of this habit.

Which is why my career in the arts is as a writer, not as a musician. I never got to "good enough" as an editor, but I could feel it looming on the horizon. I moved on before "good enough" became part of my editing vocabulary.

This is why I tell you to do a gut check *daily*. Because you'll be able to chart the progress of what you do and how you're feeling. Honestly, it's okay to discover that a dream you've had is not for you.

But here's what's not okay: it's not okay to give up on yourself because you're not worthy, or someone else has told you the task facing you is impossible.

I have a quote on the bulletin board next to my desk. It's from Thomas Carlyle: "Every noble work is at first impossible."

And another from Judy Garland: "Always be a first-rate version of yourself, rather than a second-rate version of someone else."

That's what we're talking about here. You need to be a first-rate version of yourself, and only you know who that person is. You're living your life, not your mother's life or your best friend's life. Only you know what you're capable of.

Don't do what everyone thinks you should do. Do what *you* think you should do.

And don't give up because others tell you you're not capable of success. Prove them wrong.

6. Be tenacious.

Cling to your dream. Work for your goal. If you step off the path, climb back on the moment you realize you've veered in the wrong direction.

You will make mistakes. You will take the wrong path. The key is to come back to yourself, and come back to the right road *for you*.

I can't tell you if you're giving up on yourself. Only you can know that.

Dean has one other question, and it's a big one: when you're on your deathbed, what will you regret?

Will you regret not striving hard enough for your dream? Will you regret lost years while you were succeeding in a profession other than the one you love? Will you regret being "good enough?"

Only you can answer those questions.

And you should. Daily. To keep yourself on track.

To keep yourself from giving up.

Staying Positive

I wrote sections of the *Guide* every week. Mostly, I answered questions or worked off a topic list. But the week I wrote this section, I had been dealing with some issues of my own, mostly to do with my office cat. She had lived alone in my office for more than a decade because she didn't play well with others (tried, in fact, to kill anything with fur, including raccoons). She had been quite ill, and the week I wrote this, we had finally decided it was time to end her misery.

My office will never be the same.

I took that opportunity to move my office to a new space, where I have three office kitties, and even more privacy than I had before. But it had been an emotional week for me, so I really didn't want to discuss money.

Instead, I thought I'd answer two questions, both on emotions and freelancing.

The first, from writer Michael Samerdyke, inspired the title of this section. He writes, "Will you include something on how to stay positive?"

Remaining positive sounds like such a minor thing. Yet it is the key to everything. Oddly enough, successful freelancers are the most cynical, hard-bitten optimists in the entire world.

We have to be. Who would believe in us if we didn't believe in ourselves?

No one discusses remaining positive at a day job, unless it is a requirement of that day job. When I worked as a waitress, I had to smile at the customers and be nice. It was in the job description. The same rules applied, perhaps more stringently, at my very first retail job. We had to be so incredibly nice at that store that we were required (again, as part of the job description) to wish each and every customer a very nice day.

This is not what I mean about positive.

You can grump around your home office for weeks if you want to. You can snarl at the cable news channels, like I often do (particularly during an election cycle). You can declare a book useless and toss it across the room if you like without worrying about hitting one of your co-workers, since you no longer have any.

You can be the surliest, nastiest person on Earth because you work alone. If being surly and anti-social makes you happy, then by all means, have at it.

When you work alone, you don't need rules for office behavior. If you don't receive clients in your office, like most freelancers, then you can behave any way you want to.

Most freelancers don't take this acting out very far. Mostly, they do a few cosmetic things they would never have done at the day job, like spend the entire day in sweats or in their pajamas. Some don't shower until they finish work.

Fine. Good. Whatever.

I do dress in Northwest casual to go to my office. I wear the clothes that I would wear to a restaurant or to the post office. My mother believed that appearances mattered, and that part of my upbringing rubbed off.

In fact, something she said (repeatedly) actually stuck. Dressing properly makes you feel better. And you know something? It does. I don't wear fancy clothes to the office because that feels ridiculous. But I always feel underdressed and vaguely unhappy when I wear my grubbiest clothes.

Clothing sounds like a side issue, but it's not. It's all a part of a greater whole.

A day job gives you structure. It structures your time—when you'll arrive, when you'll leave, and what you'll do while you're there. It structures your environment—someone else designs your workspace and whether you get an office with a window or a cubicle with high, carpeted walls. It structures your appearance—you may have to wear a business suit or a uniform with the company logo. Some places have strict rules about grooming. Disneyland, for example, won't allow men to have facial hair. Many restaurants I worked in didn't allow the wait staff to wear perfume, cologne or use scented soaps because those odors would interfere with the food.

Each day job, whether it's acknowledged or not, structures the employees' attitudes. Some, like the retail shops I mentioned above, required positive attitudes at all times. But most emotional structures are subtler than that. Except for discussions of last night's episode of *Lost* or some (tame) discussions of this year's baseball season, personal conversation gets discouraged.

If someone asks, "How are you today?" they really don't want to know the answer. They don't want you to launch into a litany of your ills from your aching feet to the hangover that has lingered (been encouraged?) all weekend. In fact, too much personal discussion can lead to reprimand and ultimately dismissal for inappropriate behavior.

You don't have to be positive at these jobs, but you do have to maintain some sort of professional attitude. You know once you get out of the car in the parking lot that you have to be on your best behavior until it's time to drive home.

But now, you work at home. Home, where you express every feeling, where you stay when you're sick, where you go for refuge. Home has suddenly become work, as well, and the lines have blurred.

We allowed those lines to blur long before we went full-time freelance. Before we quit our day jobs, we did our freelance work when we "felt like it" or when we "found the time" or when the muse showed up.

In the early days—for all of us—the freelance work was a side business or a hobby, something we did because we loved it or because it filled the time.

The day job, on the other hand, was something we did for the money.

Now, we freelance for the money. We forget that we used to do this sort of thing for fun. Sometimes full-time freelancing takes all the joy out of the operation.

The key isn't so much recapturing that joy—remaining joyful day after day isn't something most humans are capable of—but remembering the joy. Remembering that you are doing the work that you love and you're lucky to be doing so.

One of the best pieces of advice I ever gave one of my writing students was accidental. He was so serious about his writing that every sentence had become torture. I told him to go play. The advice stuck. He made a sign that said *Go Play* and put it across from his desk where he could see it every single day.

It didn't put him in a good mood every day, but it did help him feel better about his freelancing.

Staying positive is tough for a variety of reasons. I mentioned one in the essay on priorities. People who spend the majority of their time alone are prone to depression. Study after study has shown this.

The solutions are simple, but do take time away from the freelancing. Some are basic: Get enough rest, eat good food (not junk food), and exercise. In fact, a recent study showed that a half-hour run has the same effect on a person's mood that a single dose of Valium has. Plus the run is cheaper and has many other benefits.

You must also schedule time to be with other people, doing fun things. This sounds silly, but many freelancers spend their free time with other freelancers, discussing business. Take the time to see a movie or to go to the beach or take in a basketball game.

People whose freelancing requires little more than a computer and a wi-fi connection can go to restaurants, libraries, and other places to get some work done. One Christian writer I know spends every afternoon in a local restaurant, researching, writing, and going over his manuscripts. He eats lunch, pays a little extra for his coffee, and socializes just enough to keep his mood elevated.

It works for him. Sometimes, that solution works for me, too.

But the toughest part about staying positive has nothing to do with the lack of companionship or the right attitude. It takes focus to remain optimistic.

First, you need confidence in your work. Most of us don't have it. If pushed, we confess to all kinds of insecurities, problems, reasons why our work isn't as good as it could possibly be.

Yet we need to believe in ourselves to do a good job.

What do I recommend? Act like you have the confidence. Eventually, you'll improve in this area. I learned this through theater training. Traditional acting schools teach that if you mimic an emotion, you can actually bring that emotion out in yourself.

Think about that for a moment: Before you started freelancing full-time, you probably described your emotional life as pretty balanced. It had to be. You had to maintain a professional decorum at your day job.

Then you quit that day job, spent all your time at home, and your emotions started running amuck. You didn't have to pretend any more. You could be yourself—and yourself, like the rest of ourselves, is an emotional rollercoaster.

That rollercoaster is fine—and often good for those of us in the arts—but you have to be aware you're riding it. You need to assume that mask of professional decorum when dealing with the outside world. You need to filter all the information from the outside world through the same professional mask.

If a new client doesn't return a phone call on time, it's not because the client hates you. It's because the client didn't have time to get to the phone that day or forgot or something equally silly. But we lose track of that when we work at home, for ourselves, with no one to balance us.

Work to retain your optimism. You quit your day job because you believed you could succeed as a freelancer. You need to remember that each and every day. If that means putting a sign up in your office that says *Believe in yourself!*, then do it. Who'll see the little aphorisms you post around your desk? You're not in someone else's building any more. Your office is private, so design it in a way that keeps you motivated and happy.

That includes things like music. Or an excellent view. Or a great screen saver. (I have one that makes me smile, no matter what.) I keep a cartoon-a-day calendar, and read it every day, which also helps, believe it or not.

But the most important part of staying positive is to remain realistic. If forty-five people say something nice to us and one person says something mean, we'll remember the something mean and discount the nice things.

As freelancers, we have to keep track of the good and the bad. And we have to give them the proper weight. Teaching reminds me how to weigh the things around me. As I explain things to my writing students, I realize the things I've overlooked in my own life.

However, I do work hard to remain realistic. My first and best tool for this is my calendar. I have a *New Yorker* desk calendar, encased in leather and embossed with my name, at my right hand, just past my computer's mouse.

I write every single good thing that happens to me in a day on that calendar. I keep track of fan mail, covers, publications, awards, and the amount of money I receive.

I think getting paid for my work is a good and positive thing. Rather than relegate it all to the accounting program, I also keep track in my calendar.

I also keep track of good comments, even from people who have rejected my work.

People who work for themselves have trouble keeping track of time. First-time freelancers soon learn that they can't tell Thursday from Tuesday without help. Even if you take the weekends off, the weekdays seem remarkably the same.

Goals & Dreams

The good things that happen to you will seem far in the distance, even if they happened a week ago. The bad things, conversely, will seem like they happen every day, even if the last one happened a month before. Remember that we focus on the bad and often forget the good.

So, on bad days, I go back through my calendar and look at all the good things that have happened. It helps me maintain perspective.

I do realize that some professions don't have the regular positive feedback that my job does. Some people work for years on the same project, or they do healing work (like massage or psychotherapy) that often has no real end to it, or they work in professions with no real feedback at all.

How do you stay positive in jobs like that?

The same way you remain positive when you're just starting your business and have no real sticks to measure success with.

You have to learn how to measure success from within, not from the outside. In other words, set daily goals and reward yourself for achieving them.

The daily goals must be realistic. They can't be too easy or you'll finish in an hour and feel like you haven't worked. On the other hand, they can't be too hard or you'll never achieve them and will always feel discouraged. You must set a goal that makes you put in some effort and gives you a good result at the same time.

Writers generally set a word limit—writing so many words of new material each and every day. Musicians often set a time limit—practicing for so many hours each and every day. EBay sellers will often set a goal of making a certain number of listings each and every day.

The type of goal will vary from business to business, but it must be something that you can achieve *daily*. I also set weekly goals and monthly goals. Even though I'm very structured, I usually miss my monthly goals—something gets in the way or goes long or (as in this week) life intrudes a bit and puts me behind.

Sometimes I miss my weekly goals as well due to illness or some other interruption. But I rarely miss my daily goals, and I still reward myself for achieving them. The rewards are small—an extra hour of television that night or a brand-new paperback book or just a simple pat on the back. I mark that success in my calendar, so that I can look back on bad days and say, "Well, at least I achieved my goals in the past week."

Sometimes, that's all I need.

The other aspect to being realistic is to know your limitations. During the same week that Michael Samerdyke asked his question, Laura Ware asked something similar. Laura, a Florida columnist and freelance fiction writer, has had life intrude on her work in a very big way.

She has become the full-time caretaker for her very ill elderly in-laws. With the help of her family and an occasional visit from home health care services, she tends to her in-laws seven days per week. But Laura is determined to continue with her freelance work in the middle of all of this.

She asks, "When you're in the kind of place [that I'm in], how do you know what's slacking, what's too much, and what's appropriate?"

That's a very healthy question. Because if you set your goals too high, you'll feel bad. People whose lives have intruded on their work (not just freelancers, but everyone) suffer a lot of stress. Whether taking care of elderly parents or taking care of a newborn baby, things happen in all of our lives that cause stress and an additional burden (even if, in the case of the baby, it's a burden that we want).

What we have to do is, again, be realistic. If you're the sole breadwinner for your family, you can't drastically cut back your hours. You may have to hire outside help or work with other family members so that they can share some of the burden.

But if you're not yet a major breadwinner, if part of the condition that the family imposed on you quitting your day job was to be the stay-at-home parent or to take care of the elderly parents or, in the case of a friend of mine, to be the sole caretaker of a dying spouse, then you must shave your work goals accordingly.

You need to figure out when you can steal the hours to get work done and if you'll be in any shape to do the work when those hours happen. If you're under a great deal of stress, like Laura is, cutting back on sleep is a terrible idea. If you're just overwhelmed with car pooling and running errands, you might have to change your work habits by figuring out what parts of your job you can do on the run.

In Laura's e-mail, she adds this, "I'm tapping this out on my phone while sitting in a waiting room with my mother-in-law (she has a doctor's appointment). After I send this, I'll fire up my laptop and try to get something done while I sit around."

Laura is one of the hardest workers I know. She gets a lot done while caring for her family. She's organized and driven, and unwilling to give up her dreams, even though she's in a tough spot right now. She routinely writes five hundred words per day, which is a great deal given her situation.

Yet as her question says, she feels like she's not doing enough.

So, let's take the question bit by bit: How do you know what's slacking?

I think we all know deep down when we're not working hard enough. If we're spending most of our time watching television or playing video games, we're not working hard enough. Some people compare themselves to other freelancers and think, *I should be working as hard as they are.* That's not the answer either, because everyone is in a different circumstance.

Know your circumstance, know what you're capable of, and then make a realistic assessment of your life. Try to achieve your new daily goal for a week. If you never reach the goal, figure out if the problem is that you weren't putting in enough time, that you didn't have enough time to give (as in Laura's case), or if the goal is just too hard to achieve in a single day *for you*.

Then, set a new goal and try that for a week. Work until you find one you have to stretch just a little to achieve, but make sure it is one you can achieve. When you're ill or taking care of something in your life that takes precedence (like sickly elderly parents), then you might have to cut back on your daily goals. When you're in excellent physical shape with no distractions in your life, raise your goals. Don't set anything in concrete. Be flexible but realistic.

If you can achieve your daily goal in fifteen minutes and spend the rest of the day goofing off, you're slacking. In this case, you need to measure how much leisure time you have. If you're spending too much time recreating, and not enough creating, you're slacking.

The next part of her question: What's too much?

If you have no leisure time, if you're getting repetitive stress injuries, if the people around you whom you trust start telling you forcefully that you need time off, then you are working too much. In the last two years of our publishing company, our friends started handing Dean articles on stress management. He was putting in 20 hours per day, seven days per week, and it showed. Eventually he collapsed, and no one was surprised, except him.

He's learned how to moderate, although he doesn't like it much. I've learned that he still works harder than anyone else I know. But now he's working a more sensible schedule (10-12 hours per day, with one weekday evening and one full day per week off), and getting 8 hours of sleep per night. He occasionally thinks he's slacking, but no one gives him articles on stress management any more.

And the final part of Laura's question: What's appropriate?

Appropriate is an interesting word, because it implies that there are Standards To Be Met.

The cool thing about being a freelancer is that you set your own standards. What's appropriate for me, a person with few responsibilities and a long-term career with several obligations, isn't appropriate for Laura or for anyone else reading this.

So, let's rephrase the question in a way that Goldilocks and the Three Bears would understand: What's just right?

Just right changes. Just right may be 500 words per day because you're taking five minutes here and five minutes there. Just right might be 5,000 words per day because you have no other obligations or 8,000 words per day because you waited too long to start that book under deadline.

Goals & Dreams

For a therapist friend of mine, four days of client meetings per week was just right. It kept her fresh for her patients. She was able to maintain her emotional balance at four days, with three-day weekends to recharge. She figured out how many patients she could reasonably handle, how many she could help, and how many would drain her. And she picked the answer that allowed her to remain healthy and to do the work that helped the clients that she had.

Once you've figured out what's just right for you, then make a note of it. Set it up as a goal to be reassessed when the current situation changes. Then strive to meet that goal every single day.

And reward yourself for doing so.

Early on in your freelance career, the only good things will be subtle ones—meeting your daily goal and enjoying the work that you quit your day job to do.

The best way to remain positive is to remind yourself that you're now doing the work you love, day in and day out. Most people aren't that lucky. Most people never get the chance to do what they love.

You have taken that opportunity.

Enjoy it, and value it for what it is—something special. Something worthwhile.

An achievement, in and of itself.

Reaching For Your Dreams

Sometimes I have to wonder if I was a history major and am a science fiction writer because I see patterns in what Thomas Jefferson called "the course of human events" or if I see patterns because I had training in both history and science fiction. I suppose that's one of those unanswerable questions. But the one thing that is clear is that my mind doesn't work like other people's.

Let us pause for the expected chorus of "well, duh."

Now that the chorus has passed, let me explain why I started with that blanket statement.

I am a news junkie. I consider the news—however it gets consumed—an essential part of freelancing. Most people who pay attention to the news and stay informed get a sense of what's going on, what to expect, and why to expect it.

But they simply don't get a "course of human events" overview. Not everyone thinks that way.

So...here are the factors that have gone into my thinking when I wrote this section. An article in the *Washington Post* on November 11, 2009, about a college graduate whose "bright future" was torn away from her by the recession. The housing statistics that came out this week, which revealed that one in four American homeowners with a mortgage are underwater (meaning they owe more—much more—than the house is worth). For many who choose to (or can) stay in their homes, the houses will not regain their lost worth for another 15 years. (CBS News EconWatch blog, November 24, 2009)

That same week, the Federal Reserve predicted that the high unemployment rate would continue through 2010. Estimates vary, but the rate hovers around 10.2 percent. That 10.2 percent does not include the underemployed—people who want to work full time but can only find part-time work. If those people get included, then the rate of un- and underemployed goes to more than 17 percent. (Turns out the Fed prediction, which I found on Marketwatch.com on November 24, 2009, was right.)

Those statistics—the 25% of all Americans with a mortgage, combined with the more than 17% un- and underemployment created a perfect storm to make things worse. Because people who received a job offer out-of-state could not afford to sell their house in order to move.

Think about it. They would sell their home at a loss, then be on the hook for the difference between their mortgage and the sale price. In other words, they might sell their home and be in debt for $100,000 or more.

This led one analyst to claim that people in that situation would be better off walking away from their underwater mortgages. Better to damage your credit rating, Christopher Thornberg of Beacon Enterprises told CBS News, than it would be to continue to throw money down a black hole.

All of this came on the heels of a study that showed the herd mentality is hardwired into human beings. (PBS.org, November 11, 2009) We feel better if we do what other people are doing—*even if we know it's wrong or does not benefit us at all.*

It takes more than chutzpah to go against conventional wisdom. It takes courage and perhaps a slightly screwed-up internal wiring. Which explains even more about me.

(And there it is again: the "well, duh," chorus. We wait for the sound to pass and now continue...)

So, what does this all mean to the historian/science fiction writer in me? A lot, actually. We are in the middle of more than the Great Recession. We're in the middle of a generational shift. And even more than that, we're in one of those sweeping moments of cultural change.

Dean and I discussed it a bit before I wrote this section. The credit rating—which only matters if you're going to borrow money—will lose (and perhaps already has lost) its godlike status in the American mind. So many people did things to preserve their credit ratings. For a long time, Dean and I watched in confusion because, as freelancer writers, we realized that credit ratings had no meaning for us. Then, employers started using credit ratings as they hired people (!), and insurance companies started basing rates on credit ratings (!), and businesses stopped taking cash, requiring plastic (!) preferring credit to debit cards and...and...and...we acquiesced to the culture and actually did some work to make sure we had a credit rating, too.

Now, most people have no credit rating. Wealthy people are cutting loose second and third homes, homes that have devalued so much as to be worthless to them—thinking, like the analyst said, what's the point of pouring money into a black hole when the money could (and probably should) go elsewhere. Formerly middle class people without work are trying very hard to put food on the table, credit rating be damned. And landlords no longer use credit ratings to judge the applications for rentals because they have to keep the units filled to pay the mortgage on their (probably underwater) commercial property.

And on, and on, and on.

The credit rating is but one shift. There is also the shift in attitude toward housing. The conventional wisdom will shift from turning houses over to this: If you're going to be in an area for only a few years, you'll rent rather than buy. If you expect to stay somewhere permanently, you'll buy, but your house won't be an ATM. Your house may increase in value or it may decrease in value, but it will be the place where you live. And (oh my!) paying off the house will probably become a lot more important than getting your mortgage interest deduction.

How does all of this relate to freelancing? And how does it relate to the girl interviewed in the *Washington Post*, the girl who lost her "bright future"? And the herd mentality?

I've bemoaned an attitude that I saw in generations who were born or came of age after 1980. I knew this was a generational thing; I also realized that they would eventually understand How The World Really Works. (She writes, sounding like the old fart that she is.) But it wasn't me hoping they'll get their comeuppance, although I did worry what would happen when they finally did realize that the world is an uncertain place. It was me, trying to understand where the attitude came from, and what exactly was going on.

I didn't realize that I had part of the attitude myself until I read the article in the *Washington Post*. I didn't add the link because the article is unremarkable. But this story put things in perspective for me because it spoke to my upbringing. Like me, this girl was raised in a family that believed in higher education. And like my family, hers believed that the better the school, the better the opportunities.

Where our families diverged was only in generational experience. My father, the first person in the American branch of his family to go to college, graduated in the Depression. (That his parents could afford college in the Depression has recently helped me understand why my mother thought them wealthy. By the standards of the day—with my grandfather's regular job as a rural mail carrier, which brought in a good salary—my grandparents were well off. It wasn't just because my mother had survived on radish sandwiches and lived in the attic of a boarding house; it was because my paternal grandparents could provide my father [and later, my aunt] with opportunities most families couldn't fathom at the time.) Graduating in the Depression with a college degree opened some doors, but not others. Jobs weren't guaranteed.

Nor were they guaranteed when I graduated from college. Not that I graduated with honors from an Ivy League school. I graduated from a very good state school with an A- GPA in an area (history) that realistically held *no* opportunity for employment for someone with a bachelor's degree.

So when I read in the *Washington Post* article that the guaranteed $200,000 jobs for college graduates with business degrees had dried up in the last few years, I just about choked on my breakfast. Excuse me? Guaranteed *$200,000* jobs? Granted, the article was talking about guaranteed jobs for the A-list graduates of a top school, but still. *Guaranteed*?

Later in the week, I heard another choking statistic: that recent college graduates would have to settle for jobs that paid an average of $50,000. Where the heck would they find those jobs? And wouldn't they be crowded out of the position by unemployed people my age?

The news has been filled lately with the plight of recent college graduates. Business has finally come to its senses. With a proliferation of candidates—one company that needed 100 workers recently saw 2,000 applicants show up *in one day*—business are hiring the people with experience, people with families, and a commitment to the community. They're not hiring a hotshot straight out of the Ivy League who needs to learn how the business world works.

And they're not hiring every experienced person either—as many of you well know. It takes hundreds of submitted resumes just to get an interview, and it might take hundreds of interviews to get a job.

Like so many recent college grads, the girl in the article has stopped submitting resumes in her chosen field. Instead, she's thinking of working odd jobs, traveling, and doing what my husband's generation called "finding herself." She has been walking down a path carved out for her from childhood and has finally realized that she needs to look at other paths to see which one suits her.

All well and good. Everyone experiences that at one point or another. As I read the article, I saw opportunity. Her parents saw disaster and a "wasted" education, one they had spent hundreds of thousands of dollars on with the certainty that it would bring their child success after graduation. They blame the fact that the education isn't paying off on her for failing to submit resumes, not on the sea change that is happening around all of us.

And that's what caught me about this article, as opposed to all the other articles about all the other college students for whom the promise of a bright future has not yet been fulfilled. It was the parents' expectation that if they did A, B, and C, and their daughter did as she was told, that it would all pay off in the end.

I am of this girl's parents' generation. And while I have always believed that marching to your own drummer was the best way to go, I've seen that as an aberrant attitude, not as a sensible one. I've been a bit apologetic for my attitude, a bit militant about it, citing my rebellious nature.

What I didn't see is how an attitude that had come from a wealthy post-war period had become engrained into all of us growing up after World War II. That period of relative stability led to choices and attitudes—even in the deep recession of the 1970s—that became hardwired into everyone in the Baby Boomer Generation. Those attitudes became expectations for our children—of course we're all going to be richer, more successful, and smarter than our parents! We have better opportunities.

Those of us who turned our backs on those opportunities—on the accepted path—were considered odd. And if we didn't succeed, it was our attitude that caused us to fail or so the accepted wisdom went. Those of us who did succeed did so because we were "lucky" or "talented" or "special"—not because we took risks that paid off.

Now, we're watching an entire generation come of age for whom the rules have failed. Some of these kids will become bitter young, as the promises that they heard when they were growing up didn't get fulfilled. And some will succeed on that path they were hardwired to march along.

But the rest, the rest have an opportunity that previous generations didn't have.

The rest don't have to postpone their dreams.

They can follow their dreams because they have nothing to lose. They've already lost the "expected," "certain" path.

We might be approaching a great period of creativity and innovation in American life, creativity and innovation that wasn't born of solid steady work but of necessary risk to survive.

Because for the first time in at least fifty years, maybe more, we have a generation coming of age that has the opportunity to create their own path. The adults around them are struggling too hard to survive themselves to put the brakes on the younger generation. And any clear-eyed adult realizes that the opportunities for the inexperienced worker have dried up, no matter what their pedigree.

People born in the 1980s now have a chance to take extreme risks, to fail spectacularly and maybe, to succeed spectacularly. Because risk, for them, is different.

The Baby Boomers married in their early 20s, had children, and settled on a career that they thought would sustain them for life. Yes, there were the rebels in the late 1960s and early 1970s, but they were seen as outliers—as outsiders, in many ways—and for many of them their hippie/protest days were just a phase.

By the time Baby Boomers realized they weren't doing what they wanted to do, that they were running out of time to make a real difference in the world, to follow their passion, they had a family, a mortgage, regular bills, and a job they were afraid to sacrifice. All that work, all those promotions. They had guaranteed retirement, and they would write or paint or start a small business after the age of 65.

A lot of those Baby Boomers are coming to our writing classes now. These people are retired and they have the time, and many of them have the beginnings of a career—several story sales, a novel sale, maybe more—but they're embarking on a career that can take ten years to ramp up.

In the ten years since Dean and I did our first workshop, two of our students have died—an older man who waited until retirement to start writing, and a driven middle-aged man who had a nonfiction career and wanted to make a living at fiction. He never achieved the "make a living" part, although he sure published a lot of fiction in his last few years.

I've watched others who have postponed their dreams struggle with years of learned behavior—deference to authority, an unwillingness to rock the boat, an inability to operate outside of a corporate structure. When you get older, you feel the end of your life looming. That feeling of immortality that you had as a teenager is a long-ago memory. The feeling that anything is possible that you had in your twenties is gone. As a middle-aged adult, you know that some things are no longer possible. (As I said to one of my students: I now know I will never play professional basketball, no matter how much I want to. She laughed, but understood. Even if I had Michael Jordan's skills, I'd still be fifty—an age that no one (yet) plays professional basketball).

Postponing your dreams is a dangerous thing to do. Because time does eventually run out. In order to freelance, you need to learn how to take risks, and if you spent a lifetime on the accepted path, risks become something to avoid. Yet freelancers can't survive without it.

When you postpone your dreams, you take a risk that you'll live long enough to pursue them *and to have success*. What most people who postpone their dreams fail to realize is that when they retire, they might have the time to work on their dreams full time, but they might not have the time to achieve them.

There's more to freelancing than the skill that brought you to the table. You must learn how to manage money, how to run your own business, how to survive failure, and how to turn that failure into a success. All of that takes time. And time is the one commodity that we have that we can't count on. We really don't know if we'll get hit by a bus tomorrow. And we shouldn't bank on surviving that bus accident if it happens.

Right now, the economy is providing millions of people with the opportunity to take their destinies into their own hands. So many people postponed their dreams because they felt they had something to lose. If they quit their job, they could lose their house, their credit rating, the respect of their neighbors. They could force their family into poverty, lose their health insurance,

GOALS & DREAMS

and risk the fortunes of everyone they love, not just their own fortunes.

All of those things are excellent considerations. So many people had to postpone their dreams. One friend of mine got pregnant in high school and spent twenty years raising children, barely eking out a living as a single mom. She postponed her dreams out of necessity, and as soon as the kids moved out of the house, she pursued those dreams with great purpose—and is having great success.

Like her, many of you had no choice. You had to postpone.

But the world has changed. Attitudes have changed *and will remain changed for decades to come.* The credit rating will no longer be so important. No one cares who pays their bills because everyone is struggling right now.

And if you've lost your job, you've already lost your steady income. You're probably juggling bills, trying to survive. Continue to send out resumes, but as you do, consider following your dreams. Because all those things you would have jeopardized ten years ago, when the economy seemed stable, are already in jeopardy.

In other words, you may have very little to lose by trying. And that's an *opportunity* just waiting to happen.

This section, though, is also aimed at newly minted college grads who have just realized that they were walking a path that now has a giant roadblock running across it. The easy road is gone. Those $200,000 jobs for you business graduates from Ivy League schools evaporated with the Wall Street meltdown.

Time to look around, to see if the road you're walking is really the one you want to be on. Even if the roadblock goes away, do you want to be a corporate executive? Do you want to work for someone else for the rest of your life? Do you dream of being a musician or a bookstore owner?

Now is the time to start. The economic collapse has instituted a sea change. People who've just graduated from college are in the same boat I was in when I graduated. I never expected to own a home (and I figured that if by some odd chance I bought one, I'd live in it for the rest of my life, so I had best be certain that was the house I wanted). I figured I would move from job to job because careers were hard to come by, especially for college grads. I started writing because I liked it—and I had nothing to lose by trying.

Whenever I use that phrase "nothing to lose," I hear the voice of my husband. Dean and I met at a writers' workshop in Taos, New Mexico, in 1986. After the workshop, we both went home—me to Wisconsin, and Dean to Idaho. Within the week, he was driving to Wisconsin to be with me.

I asked him why. We loved each other and had planned to get together in August, after we had settled everything in our lives. We weren't sure where we would be, but we figured we'd work it out by then.

But he went back to Idaho, to the small apartment he had moved into after he had separated from his wife, to the bartending job he had put on hold to go to the writers' workshop, and realized that nothing held him in that small town.

He said to me on the phone from some rest stop somewhere between Idaho and Wisconsin, "I'm coming to you because I have nothing to lose—"

As he said that phrase, I remember thinking, *That's worrisome. He's not coming toward something; he's coming because he has nothing else.* I heard that phrase through the filter of my upbringing: that a person with nothing to lose has failed somehow.

Then he added the important part of the sentence. It wasn't an afterthought for him. It was the central part of his message.

"—and," he said, "I have everything to gain."

He had weighed the risks against the rewards and realized he was taking no risk at all. He had no risk except the drive itself and a possible rejection by me. (Yeah, right. Like that would have happened. Not.) He had—we had—everything to gain from his willingness to start our relationship immediately.

And twenty-four years later, it's clear he was right. We have gained a great deal because he was savvy enough to realize that he was in the position to do something he wouldn't normally have been able to do.

So many of you are in that position now. Sometimes life forces us to postpone our dreams. Sometimes we postpone them out of fear.

Right now, life—and the economy—is giving millions of us nothing to lose, and everything to gain.

If we only try.

Try.

Your life will be richer if you do.

Newsletter Sign-up

I value honest feedback, and would love to hear your opinion in a review, if you're so inclined, on your favorite book retailer's site.

Be the first to know!

Please sign up for the Kristine Kathryn Rusch newsletter, and receive exclusive content, keep up with the latest news, releases and so much more—even the occasional giveaway.

So, what are you waiting for? To sign up go to kristinekathrynrusch.com.

But wait! There's more. Sign up for the WMG Publishing newsletter, too, and get the latest news and releases from all of the WMG authors and lines, including Kristine Grayson, Kris Nelscott, Dean Wesley Smith, *Fiction River: An Original Anthology Magazine, Smith's Monthly,* and so much more.

To sign up go to wmgpublishing.com.

About the Author

New York Times bestselling author Kristine Kathryn Rusch writes in almost every genre. Generally, she uses her real name (Rusch) for most of her writing. Under that name, she publishes bestselling science fiction and fantasy, award-winning mysteries, acclaimed mainstream fiction, controversial nonfiction, and the occasional romance. Her novels have made bestseller lists around the world and her short fiction has appeared in eighteen best of the year collections. She has won more than twenty-five awards for her fiction, including the Hugo, *Le Prix Imaginales*, the *Asimov's* Readers Choice award, and the *Ellery Queen Mystery Magazine* Readers Choice Award.

Publications from *The Chicago Tribune* to *Booklist* have included her Kris Nelscott mystery novels in their top-ten-best mystery novels of the year. The Nelscott books have received nominations for almost every award in the mystery field, including the best novel Edgar Award, and the Shamus Award.

She writes goofy romance novels as award-winner Kristine Grayson.

She also edits. Beginning with work at the innovative publishing company, Pulphouse, followed by her award-winning tenure at *The Magazine of Fantasy & Science Fiction*, she took fifteen years off before returning to editing with the original anthology series *Fiction River*, published by WMG Publishing. She acts as series editor with her husband, writer Dean Wesley Smith, and edits at least two anthologies in the series per year on her own.

To keep up with everything she does, go to kriswrites.com and sign up for her newsletter. To track her many pen names and series, see their individual websites:

krisnelscott.com, kristinegrayson.com, retrievalartist.com, divingintothewreck.com.

Keep informed:
www.kriswrites.com

Printed in the USA
CPSIA information can be obtained
at www.ICGtesting.com
LVHW041041291023
762469LV00004B/726